grow your own food

grow
your own food

Bath · New York · Singapore · Hong Kong · Cologne · Delhi · Melbourne

First published by Parragon in 2010

Parragon
Queen Street House
4 Queen Street
Bath BA1 1HE, UK

Copyright © Parragon Books Ltd 2010

ISBN: 978-1-4075-9074-5

Printed in China

Created and produced by Ivy Contract

The views expressed in this book are those of the author but they
are general views only. The varieties that are listed and guidance
provided are suitable for US climate zones 5–9 (please refer to US
Department of Agriculture Miscellaneous Publication 814, Plant
Hardiness Zone Map, www.usna.usda.gov/Hardzone/index.html),
but the reader should check with local nurseries for growing advice
for their own location. Parragon hereby excludes all liability to the
extent permitted by law for any errors or omissions in this book
and for any loss, damage or expense suffered by a third party
relying on any information contained in this book.

Contents

Introduction

One of the best things about gardening is being able to enjoy the fruits of your labor and perhaps nowhere is this more true than growing your own food. It's hard to beat the sense of achievement you get from picking crops from your garden and then enjoying their delicious taste and freshness. Whether you have a large plot or a small garden, a patio or even just a window box, there are herbs, vegetables, and fruit that everyone can grow.

Growing your own produce is becoming increasingly popular. This is partly because people want to know where their food comes from and to reduce the environmental damage caused by food being transported many thousands of miles around the world,

but also because it is the best way of ensuring you are getting the freshest possible nutrients and—most importantly—that unbeatable homegrown flavor.

What to grow?

Choosing which crops to grow requires some careful thought. Most vegetables are annuals, so they will have to be grown from seed or bought as small plants each year. Although this is quite labor-intensive it does mean that each year you can review what worked and what didn't, or maybe try something completely different the following year.

A good place to start is to think about where you are going to grow vegetables and fruit. Most vegetables prefer lots of sun and shelter, although there are a few that will tolerate some shade, such as spinach and lettuce. Most tree fruit, such as peaches, and nectarines, grows best against a warm, sunny wall although apples are happy in quite cold and shady conditions. You also need to grow the right vegetables for your type of soil. For example, root crops prefer a loose sandy soil while brassicas like an alkaline soil.

It is important also to consider which fruit and vegetables you actually enjoy. There is no point ending up with a beautiful row of succulent beet if your family dislikes it! Also, it is a good idea to try to grow produce that is either expensive to buy or hard to get hold of, such as young fava beans or some of the more unusual squashes.

Get to know your soil conditions to find out what grows best: in time you will be pulling up vegetables all year round.

How much to grow?

You can easily start off with a few containers or a small area of your garden. However, if you want to become truly self-sufficient, you must be prepared to invest plenty of space, time, and care. You will also need to plan carefully, as it is very easy to end up with gluts of fruit and vegetables that you can't keep up with. Conversely, you may find the winter and early spring are periods when there is little available.

Getting started

Once you have selected the area or containers that you are going to use, the next step is to remove all weeds and prepare the soil. Good soil promotes healthy plant growth. Leaf mold, composted bark, and garden compost can be dug into the soil or spread across the surface. Their bulk will improve the drainage of heavy soil and allow dry soil to hold onto moisture and nutrients.

Making your own compost is easy. Green materials such as vegetable peelings, tea bags, and grass clippings (but not weeds) mixed with brown materials, such as twigs and cardboard, will produce a nutrient-rich compost.

Growing organically

Many gardeners nowadays prefer to use organic gardening techniques instead of chemicals and fertilizers. Not only is this healthier for you, it is far better for the environment so you'll reap the benefits long term. To avoid using herbicides, you can prevent weeds by spreading bark mulch, leaf mold, or a weed prevention membrane across the soil. If weeds do appear, then try and dig them out before they set seed.

For pest problems, you can use biological controls instead of chemical sprays. There are many available commercially, such as parasitic

Food and flowers don't have to be mutually exclusive; in fact, grown together they look most attractive.

wasps that can be used to control whitefly in greenhouses and a tiny worm that kills vine weevil grubs. In addition, you can enlist the help of nature by creating the right habitats to attract natural predators to your garden. Toads will happily devour slugs and snails, while lacewings and ladybugs will relish a diet of aphids.

In this book, we will guide you through planning your plot and give you tips and advice on how to grow some of the most popular vegetables, herbs, and fruit. The second section of the book explains the seasonal tasks that will keep your kitchen garden in top condition. There are also delicious recipes throughout the book to help you make the most of your freshly harvested produce.

FOOD GARDENS

planning and preparation
starting a kitchen garden

There's no denying that growing vegetables, herbs, and some types of fruit for the kitchen takes time and trouble. But this is more than compensated for by the pleasure it gives. This is an orderly way of gardening that many people find not only intensely rewarding, but also very relaxing.

Planning and preparing

For the kitchen garden there are three main types of vegetable crop you need to plan for: root vegetables (eg beet, carrots, radishes), brassicas (eg cabbages, sprouts, and broccoli), and legumes (podded vegetables such as peas and beans). The onion family can be given a permanent plot or can be put in along with the legumes. Leeks, which are planted at a different time from most vegetables, can be put in as and where there is space. Lettuces can be planted with the roots or legumes and can also go in as "catch crops," to be picked as their neighbors grow and need the space.

This kitchen garden has raised beds which help to provide good drainage and warm the soil.

Preparing the plot

Vegetables are greedy feeders, so the soil needs to be well prepared before you plant. Ideally you should dig it over well in the fall before you begin and lay a thick layer of manure or garden compost on top (or dig it in); then fork over again in the spring. Finally, rake the beds to prepare them for seeds and seedlings.

Reasons for rotating

It is important to move types of crop from area to area to discourage the buildup of

crop rotation			
	BED A	BED B	BED C
Year 1	Brassicas	Roots	Legumes
Year 2	Legumes	Brassicas	Roots
Year 3	Roots	Legumes	Brassicas
Year 4	Brassicas	Roots	Legumes

If you don't have the time or the space for a dedicated kitchen garden, you can still grow occasional vegetables and herbs among your flower borders.

pests and diseases. There are diseases and predators for almost all plants, but they are far less likely to become established if the crop varies from year to year.

Different types of vegetables also have their own particular requirements, as well as having specific effects on the soil. Peas and beans, the legumes most commonly grown in the kitchen garden, enrich the soil by fixing nitrogen, which is needed by brassicas and leafy vegetables, while root crops improve the soil for the legumes. Root crops do best where manure was applied for the previous growing season. Too rich a soil makes them fork under the ground and produce leaf instead of root.

A well-stocked kitchen garden with ornamental herbs and vegetables provides a feast for the eye as well as for the table.

The best way of rotating crops in your kitchen garden is to divide the plot into three areas and grow brassicas in bed A, root crops in bed B, and legumes in bed C. The following year, legumes move into bed A, brassicas into bed B, roots into bed C, and so on. This means that the bed with roots can be manured at the end of the season ready for the brassicas, while the roots have nitrogen fixed in the soil from the legumes of the previous year.

planning and preparation
designing a kitchen garden

When planning your kitchen garden, think about the site and its exposure to ensure you get the best growing conditions. The ideal is a south-facing, sheltered area. Remember to include space for flowers as they attract beneficial insects and provide color.

Sample design

The plot selected to be turned into a kitchen garden is south facing and open, with terraces that could form the basis for the vegetable beds.

Each terrace is leveled using a rototiller, to avoid the seeds being washed away by the first rainstorm. The ground should be cleared of stones, weeds, and debris and the soil raked to a fine tilth. The brick retaining walls are best replaced with low walls of new, tanalized, or reclaimed railway ties, supported at regular intervals by sawn timber posts. Paths can be laid with bark mulch to intersect the beds and provide a soft but firm surface, as well as easy access for tending and harvesting the plants. Trellis panels can be fixed over sloped banks to help climbers.

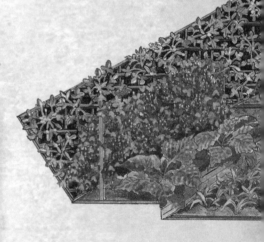

Ideally, a kitchen garden needs an open site in full sun: fences and walls quickly cast shade on a small plot. Make sure you allow plenty of access to the crops, to avoid walking on the beds and compacting the soil.

A pot of bright pelargoniums.

❶ Compost

Compost bins are hidden from view.

❸ Bark path

Paths are covered with bark chippings.

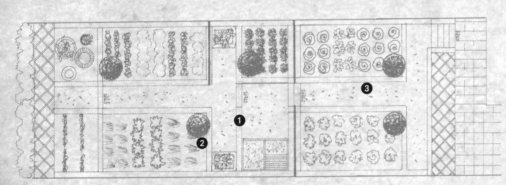

-50ft x 16ft/15m x 5m-

growing vegetables
root vegetables and bulb crops

Beet, carrots, parsnips, and potatoes are all root crops. Onions, shallots, garlic, and leeks are all bulb crops. Roots and bulbs offer a lengthy harvesting period, some of it during the fall and winter and, for the most part, a long storage life. They also produce a large amount of food in a small amount of space.

Beet—a delicious, highly nutritious vegetable and when eaten fresh with butter and garlic, beet is a culinary delight. Sow outdoors from mid-spring onward when the soil has warmed up. Soak the seed overnight before sowing and it will germinate in 10–14 days.

Carrots—like peas, a fresh carrot tastes far better than any you can buy. Seed should be sown very thinly in situ. If you wish, you can sow seed in modules and then plant them out in position. If you have space, sow them at two-weekly intervals to produce a succession of crops.

Potatoes—these tubers, the swollen roots of the plant, are well worth having in your kitchen garden. Potatoes must be grown from seed potatoes, not ones bought from a supermarket as they can carry viruses. For an early crop, put the potatoes on a cool windowsill until sprouts have begun to form (a process known as "chitting") before planting them outside from early spring onward.

Potatoes need to be planted about 5in/13cm deep in rows about 30in/75cm apart. Once the first leaves appear, the plants need to be covered in earth if you live in an area where frosts occur. Cold-stored potatoes can also be planted in the summer to give a crop in the fall.

The many varieties of potatoes are often categorized according to their season: early, mid, or maincrop.

Onions of any sort are a kitchen staple: grow as many as you can!

Parsnips—these are easy root crops to grow and because they can stay in the soil over winter, particularly if you cover them with a layer of straw, they make an excellent choice if you want your garden to produce all year.

The best soil for parsnips is rich, well-drained but not too light or stony. As with many root crops, it should not be recently manured as this causes the parsnip to fork. Parsnips can be sown direct into the ground in the late winter or early spring. They should be sown into drills at a depth of ¾in/2cm. The rows should be 10in/25cm apart.

Onions/shallots—both of these are bulb not root crops but are included here as they can be grown with root crops (or legumes). Onions and shallots are grown from "sets," which are tiny bulbs.

sicilian stuffed tomatoes

serves 4

8 large ripe tomatoes. 7 tbsp extra virgin olive oil. 2 onions, finely chopped. 2 garlic cloves, crushed. 2 cups fresh bread crumbs. 8 anchovy fillets in oil, drained and chopped. 3 tbsp black olives, pitted and chopped. 2 tbsp chopped fresh flat-leaf parsley. 1 tbsp chopped fresh oregano. 4 tbsp freshly grated Parmesan cheese

Preheat the oven to 350°F/180°C. Cut a thin slice off the tops of the tomatoes and discard. Scoop out the seeds with a teaspoon and discard, taking care not to pierce the shells. Turn the tomato shells upside down on paper towels to drain.

Heat 6 tablespoons of the oil in a skillet, add the onions and garlic, and cook over low heat, stirring occasionally, for 5 minutes, until softened. Remove the skillet from the heat and stir in the bread crumbs, anchovies, olives, and herbs.

Using a teaspoon, fill the tomato shells with the bread crumb mixture, then arrange them in a single layer in a large ovenproof dish. Sprinkle the tops with grated Parmesan and drizzle with the remaining oil.

Bake in the preheated oven for 20–25 minutes, until the tomatoes are tender and the topping is golden brown. Serve immediately.

They should be planted in mid-spring in rows about 6in/15cm apart, pressed into a shallow drill, so their tips just show when firmed in. If you want an early spring crop, you can try planting some of the more unusual Japanese varieties in late summer.

A single shallot set will divide to produce a crop of small bulbs so these are good value for money.

Garlic—fresh garlic has an unbeatable taste and texture. Like onions and shallots, garlic is a bulb crop. It needs to grow quickly in order to produce good-sized bulbs so plant it in a sunny spot that is well drained to ensure the bulbs do not rot during the winter. It's an easy crop to grow, requiring only the addition of some fertilizer in spring and watering during dry spells.

Garlic is normally ready for harvesting when most of the foliage has turned from green to a yellowy-brown color—this will usually be from mid- to late summer.

top tip

To add some spice to your roast potatoes, mix together 1 tsp chili powder, ½ tsp caraway seeds, and 1 tsp salt. Sprinkle the mixture over the potatoes just before roasting.

growing vegetables
legumes and other rotation crops

Legumes include peas and beans. Although beans are easy to grow, peas can be more tricky but the taste of fresh peas makes the effort worthwhile. For the purposes of a three-bed rotation, squash, pumpkins, leeks, tomatoes, eggplants, zucchini, and cucumbers are included as they are not brassicas or root crops.

Peas—peas are one of the commonest and most loved garden vegetables, but they can be frustratingly difficult to grow because they are popular with birds and mice. They can be difficult to germinate, too, because they do not relish cold soils, and conversely they are a cool-weather crop and dislike open hot positions. When ripe, peas should be cooked immediately after picking as the sugar starts to turn to starch once the pod has been picked. Peas can be sown in succession to maintain a regular supply over the summer.

Beans—these can grow as either a pole or a bush bean. Dwarf beans grow as small bushy plants close to the ground, and need no support. Pole beans need the support of canes, trellis, or a fence as they can get quite tall. Pole beans can be very productive

Peas can be quite hard to grow. The variety 'Onward' is very popular among gardeners as it is ideal for successional sowing, has plenty of flavor, needs little support, and yields a very heavy crop.

over a long period of time. Beans are best grown on very fertile soil and they must be picked continually once the pods start to form. They also need plenty of water. Beans can be sown direct into the ground in late fall for an early or mid-spring crop. If you live in a frost-prone area, the young plants can be started off in a greenhouse and planted out once all risk of frost is over.

Squash/pumpkins—these are vigorous plants, so make sure you plant them where they have plenty of room to spread. If you're short of space, try a trailing variety that can be grown up a trellis or over an arch. Squash need plenty of sun and a well-drained, organic-rich soil. They can't tolerate frost so it is best to start them off in a greenhouse before planting them outside if you live in a frost-prone area. Keep them well-watered. Some squash varieties will be ready for eating in summer but most are harvested in early fall.

Winter squash should store well for weeks, but any that are damaged should be used up straightaway as they will only rot in store.

Leeks—leeks are an easy vegetable to grow. Sow them in shallow rows in early spring in a seedbed or a tray and when the seedlings are large enough to handle in midsummer, transplant them to their final positions. Make a deep hole and water the leeks in. They prefer a sunny, sheltered site with well-drained soil and need plenty of feeding. Because leeks last well into the winter, they make a good choice for the kitchen garden when little else remains in the ground.

Tomatoes—tomatoes can be grown in a greenhouse or outdoors. They do best in a relatively warm climate and are difficult to grow in open soil unless they are given the protection of a south-facing wall and a sheltered position.

Tomatoes can be divided into two types: bush and cordon. Cordon are the most common and to be successful they need to be trained up a stake or tied in to wires. Use garden string or raffia and tie in the plants at regular intervals with a loose knot. You also need to pinch out all side-shoots where the leaf stalks join the stem. This leaves you with one straight stem and a number of trusses of fruit.

When the fourth truss has small tomatoes the growing tip should be pinched out, or "stopped" at two leaves above the truss. This allows the tomatoes to develop properly and ripen well.

Cordon tomatoes can be grown in large pots or in a growing bag. If grown in pots the tall stems need to be supported with bamboo canes, but for plants grown in a bag, a supporting frame-work is better. Allow two plants per standard-size bag.

If by any chance the summer ends rather earlier than it should, and you are left with a large number of green tomatoes, they can be picked and taken inside the house to ripen on a sunny windowsill. Alternatively, use them to make a delicious green tomato chutney, a relish prized above many others (see recipe tip below).

Bush tomatoes grow either as small bushes or trailing on the ground. They require no training or stopping, but need the ground covering to keep the fruit off the soil.

Peppers—varieties of this tropical plant have been developed to thrive outside the tropics. Peppers can now be grown in a greenhouse, or outdoors (see also p.24).

staking and tying cordon tomatoes

1 Standard tomatoes can be grown in pots trained up 4ft/1.2m stakes. If possible, run a wire along the wall behind and secure the stakes to this.

2 As the tomato plants grow, tie in the leading growth and pinch out the side-shoots at the joint of the branches and main stem. Water well.

3 When the tomato has set four trusses, or reached the top of its stake, nip out the growing point two leaves above the top truss. Feed well.

in the greenhouse

There are many advantages to having a greenhouse. It allows you to control the growing environment, whatever climate zone you live in. Plants benefit from the light entering through the glass, and the daytime heat trapped inside will continue to boost the growth overnight if the greenhouse is kept closed. Gardening in a greenhouse extends the range of plants you can produce, as well as the growing season, because you can start earlier in the spring and be harvesting well into fall. This is especially desirable in cooler climates where the growing season is too short or unreliable for many plants.

The greenhouse is most commonly used to germinate seeds or produce plump juicy tomatoes but there are several other tasty crops that are worth growing: if you have room, try bell peppers, chiles, and eggplants as well as cucumbers and melons, which can be trained to twine upward, making the most of the available space. You can also sow pumpkin and squash seeds in early spring to protect them from frost, before transplanting to the open in summer.

Apart from shielding your plants from cold, windy, or wet conditions, a greenhouse protects them from attack by some pests, though you still need to watch for red spider mite and whitefly, and respond to any signs of disease. To reduce the maintenance, it pays to invest in some of the automated systems now available, such as humidity and temperature controls, and sprinklers to keep the soil moist.

top tip

You can make a spicy tomato chutney by combining 3–4 large tomatoes, 1 hot green chile, 1 tsp chili powder, and 1 small chopped onion in a blender until finely chopped. Pour into a saucepan and add 1 garlic clove, 1 tsp salt, a chunk of gingerroot, scant 2/3 cup granulated sugar, 1/2 cup cider vinegar, 3/4 cup golden raisins. Simmer uncovered until thickened—do ensure you reduce the liquids long enough, otherwise the chutney will be runny. Store in glass jars in the refrigerator.

Outdoor or ridge cucumbers are easy to grow and the plants will produce a plentiful supply in a rich, fertile soil.

Cucumbers—can be grown in greenhouses or outdoors. The latter are known as ridge cucumbers and are easily grown in fertile, moisture-retentive soil in a warm, sunny and sheltered position.

In mid-spring dig a hole 12in/30cm deep and wide. Fill it with a mixture of equal parts of topsoil and compost, and make a mound of soil on the surface. In late spring, sow three seeds ¾in/2cm deep and 2in/5cm apart. Water and cover with a large jar. Water regularly and after germination remove the cover. Later, remove the two weakest seedlings. When side-shoots have five or six leaves, pinch out their tips to just beyond a leaf joint. Water regularly, and feed when the first cucumbers start to swell.

Zucchini—Zucchini grown in the garden are far better to eat than any bought in a store. The best ones to grow are the compact bush varieties and, provided you pick regularly, the plant will continue to produce fruit over a long period.

The seeds will germinate at 59°F/15°C so zucchini are raised in pots in a greenhouse first, and then planted out when the soil has warmed up. Plants grown in pots may need to be hardened off by putting them outside during the day (and put under cover at night) before finally planted in position in the container.

Eggplants—eggplants are tropical plants, so need warm soil and high temperatures. In temperate areas many varieties can be grown in greenhouses or containers. If grown outside, make sure they are in a sheltered, sunny position in fertile, well-drained soil. The plants need to be watered regularly, otherwise the fruits will be small and bitter.

zucchini salad

serves 4-6

about 4 tbsp olive oil. 1 large garlic clove, halved. 1lb 2oz/500g small zucchini, thinly sliced. 1/3 cup pine nuts. 1/3 cup raisins. 3 tbsp finely chopped mint leaves, plus extra sprigs for garnishing. 2 tbsp lemon juice, or to taste. salt and pepper

Heat the oil in a large skillet over medium heat. Add the garlic and cook until golden. Then remove and discard. Add the zucchini and cook, stirring, until tender. Immediately remove and transfer to a large serving bowl.

Add the pine nuts, raisins, mint, lemon juice, and salt and pepper to taste and stir.

Taste and add more oil, lemon juice, and seasoning, if necessary.

Set aside and let cool. Cover and chill in the refrigerator for at least 3½ hours. Remove 10 minutes before serving. Garnish with mint sprigs to serve.

growing vegetables
brassicas and leaf vegetables

Brassicas are known as greedy crops (or gross feeders) because they take a high level of nutrients, particularly nitrogen, from the soil. Brassicas are also prone to certain pests and diseases, such as clubroot, which can remain in the soil, hence the need for rotation.

Cabbages—these very hardy members of the brassica family are a suitable choice for most temperate climates and a range of soils. Cabbages require minimal attention. Sow summer, fall, and winter cabbages thinly in succession between early spring and early summer. Sow spring cabbages in late summer for an early crop.

Cauliflowers—one of the trickier vegetables to grow well, cauliflowers need a rich, heavy soil with plenty of organic matter worked in. They grow best in full sun, as any partial shade will reduce head size. Start the plants indoors in early spring if you are in an area that has frosts. Young plants can withstand a light frost but a severe one may cause the plant to form a "button," not a full-sized head. If you want a late fall harvest, you can also plant them out in late summer. Cauliflowers

To get white cauliflower heads (curds) you will need to bend the leaves over the top.

require plenty of moisture which is best achieved by mulching.

Brussels sprouts—sprouts grow over a long season and, like most brassicas, they prefer cool conditions: they are one of the few crops that taste better after a slight frost. In warmer regions Brussels sprouts are best grown as a fall crop. Otherwise, sow in a seedbed

cauliflower & broccoli tart

serves 4

3¹/₂oz/100g cauliflower florets. 3¹/₂oz/100g broccoli florets. 1 onion, cut into 8 wedges. 2 tbsp butter or margarine. 1 tbsp all-purpose flour. 6 tbsp vegetable stock. ¹/₂ cup milk. 3oz/85g cheddar cheese, grated. 7-inch/18-cm pastry shell. salt and pepper.

Preheat the oven to 375°F/190°C.

Bring a saucepan of lightly salted water to a boil and cook the cauliflower, broccoli, and onion for about 10-12 minutes until tender. Drain and set aside.

Melt the butter in a saucepan. Add the flour and cook, stirring, for 1 minute. Remove from the heat, stir in the stock and milk, and return to the heat. Bring to a boil, stirring constantly, and add ⁴/₄ cups of the cheese. Season to taste with salt and pepper. Spoon the vegetables into the pastry shell. Pour over the sauce and sprinkle with the remaining grated cheese.

Bake in the preheated oven for 10 minutes until the cheese is golden and bubbling.

in early spring then, after thinning, plant them out in early summer into their final positions. As the plants grow, tie them to a stake, so they don't blow over in the winter.

Calabrese/broccoli—calabrese (usually sold as broccoli) can be sown directly from early to late spring until late summer. Sow in drills ½in/1cm deep and water in. Seedlings should appear in 1–2 weeks. Thin, to leave 12in/30cm between plants, to allow room for the heads to grow. Broccoli can also be sown in pots from mid-spring to midsummer.

When the seedlings are 3in/7.5cm high, plant outside in a drill 1in/2.5cm deep as they can grow quite tall.

Kohlrabi, turnips—these fast-growing brassicas can be used raw in salads or cooked in stir-fries. Sow very thinly ½in/1cm deep in rows 12in/30cm apart, then cover with soil and water. They can be sown between early spring and summer or, for a late fall or winter crop, sow in late summer. They take about 10 weeks to mature, but do pick them when the plants are young, otherwise they can become tough.

Spinach—this is included in the brassicas group because it too is a hungry crop. For a summer crop, spinach can be sown from early spring to midsummer—sow seeds 1in/2.5cm apart in trenches ½in/1cm deep, cover, and water. New rows should be about 12in/30cm apart. For a constant supply, try sowing a new row about every three weeks. Cut the leaves from the outside of the plant to ensure that plenty of new leaves will be produced.

Swiss chard—an attractive choice for the kitchen garden, Swiss chard will grow in a sunny or slightly shaded spot in fertile, moisture-retentive soil. It is usually sown in the spring for harvesting in the summer. To sow chard, make a trench 1in/2.5cm deep and then space seeds about 3¼in/8cm apart. Cover and water well. Leaves are ready to be picked 8–12 weeks after sowing.

Swiss chard or rhubarb chard is grown for its brightly colored stems and glossy leaves that can be cooked and eaten as spinach.

growing vegetables
salad crops

Salad crops are popular and easily grown; and there are many interesting and colorful varieties to choose from. They are often known as "catch crops" because they are generally fast-growing and can be easily slotted in wherever there is space that can be filled between other crops.

Lettuces—the range of types includes butterheads (cabbagelike, with large, soft, smooth-edged leaves); crispheads (another cabbage-type, with rounded heads and curled and crisp leaves); romaine lettuces (upright growth and oblong heads); and looseleaf lettuces (loose, wavy-edged leaves that are picked individually).

By sowing seeds at various times, lettuces can be harvested throughout most of the year, though summer-sown lettuces are the easiest to grow. From mid-spring to the early part of late summer, sow seeds thinly and evenly in ½in/1cm-deep drills 10in/25cm apart. Keep the area moist. When seedlings are about 1in/2.5cm high, thin them first to 4in/10cm apart and later to 12in/30cm. Thin small varieties to 10in/25cm apart. Harvest the lettuces from the latter part of early summer to fall.

Radishes—although a root vegetable, radishes are grown as a salad ingredient. They are extremely easy and quick to grow, which means they are one of the best ways to

Vegetables can be grown in even the smallest garden. Where possible, choose moderately vigorous varieties.

introduce children to the delights of gardening.

Radishes germinate easily, and mature quickly, usually in about a month. Gardeners with large kitchen gardens often use them as a marker crop between rows of vegetables that take longer to germinate, and for the adventurous there are several winter-maturing radishes and the giant Japanese daikon radishes.

mature lettuce

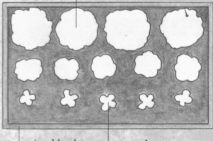
raised bed   young lettuce

Sow lettuce seeds in succession to ensure a continuous, fresh supply in summer. Try looseleaf varieties such as the popular green or purple Oakleaf lettuce for a change.

From mid-spring to late summer, sow seeds evenly and thinly every two weeks. Form drills about ½in/1cm deep and 6in/15cm apart. Germination takes 5–7 days and when the seedlings are large enough to handle, thin them to 1in/2.5cm apart. Refirm the soil around them and water it. Harvest the radishes while they are young; if left, they become woody.

Scallions—in addition to bulbing types, there are scallions, also known as green onions or bunching onions. They are quick-growing, so they are ideal for filling any gaps between slower growing crops. They need a rich, well-drained soil and are usually grown in rows 6in/15cm apart. They can just be thinly scattered in a patch and either raked in or covered with ½in/1cm of fine soil. Successionally sow each week or two from early spring for a continuous supply throughout the summer months.

Salad greens—dark green, extra tender leaves add a piquant flavor to sandwiches and salads. Just a few leaves of arugula, corn salad, or land cress will lend a tasty, peppery sharpness. Sow from mid-spring onward for a continuous harvest.

Kitchen gardens can be highly decorative as well as productive. In cottage gardens vegetables can also be grown alongside flowers.

For more variety sow mesclun, a mixture of salad greens. The seed comes ready mixed to be sown at two-weekly intervals for a continuous supply of tender leaves. Growth is rapid: leaves are ready to harvest within about three weeks.

salad of greens with lemon dressing

Serves 4

7oz/200g mixed baby salad greens such as corn salad, spinach, watercress, and wild arugula. 4 tbsp mixed chopped fresh herbs such as flat-leaf parsley, mint, cilantro, and basil. 4 tbsp extra virgin olive oil. juice of lemon. 1 garlic clove, crushed. salt and pepper

Wash the salad greens and discard any thick stalks. Dry and put in a salad bowl. Add the chopped herbs.

Mix together the oil, lemon juice, garlic, and salt and pepper in a small bowl. Taste and add more oil or lemon juice if necessary.

Just before serving, whisk the dressing; pour over the salad greens, toss, and serve.

growing vegetables
vegetables for containers

In the limited space of a container garden it is best to concentrate on your favorite vegetables: they will taste far better than anything you can buy in the stores. Grow quick-maturing crops, "mini" vegetables and unusual vegetables for special occasions.

Growing vegetables in containers is a great solution if you are short of space and a few pots just outside the door also offers convenience to those with larger gardens. Containers devoted to vegetables need very careful planning, though. Space is limited and there will only be room to raise a few plants of each vegetable. Check on the amount of room each variety requires, and try to get seed for the smaller varieties or grow the "mini" vegetables designed for containers.

Also grow those that will give you the greatest yield in the smallest space. Growing bags are a good alternative to pots if space is short.

Beet—the leaves and colorful stalks are most decorative so beet looks attractive on a patio garden or courtyard.

Bell peppers—the new, hardier varieties of this tropical fruit make good plants to grow in containers outside on a warm, sheltered patio. They are popular as a vegetable in salads, as well as roasted or stuffed. In areas prone to frost, sow the seed in mid-spring either indoors or in a greenhouse at 70°F/21°C. The seeds will germinate in 14–21 days.

Cabbages—cabbage might not be everyone's choice for growing in the limited space available in a container

garden, but it is considerably more compact than most brassicas, and a number of the red and savoy cabbages are attractive plants.

Carrots—to grow carrots in containers you need to look for short, thick varieties, rather than the larger winter ones that take longer to mature. Also aim to give the carrots as much depth as possible because they will not grow well in a shallow bag.

Cucumbers—the modern varieties of outdoor or ridge cucumbers are tolerant of lower temperatures and will grow well in containers. Plant the seeds on their edge in degradable pots, or—better still—directly into the containers outside because cucumber plants do not respond well to being transplanted. The seeds germinate at 68°F/20°C.

top tip

Make a summery dip by peeling and grating 1 small cucumber, squeezing out any excess water. Mix together with some yogurt, garlic, and chopped mint and chill in the refrigerator for 2 hours. Serve with warmed pita bread.

Crops grown in containers will suffer if the soil dries out so check its condition daily in hot weather.

Lettuces—a good standby for the container gardener. Lettuces mature quickly, require little room and can be grown easily in between other vegetables. They can also be planted to take the place of crops that have already been harvested. Sow two seeds in a small degradable pot, using as many small pots as necessary. Discard the weaker seedling if both germinate. It may be necessary to harden off the plants by putting them outside during the day before planting out in their final position outdoors.

Peas—these can be grown successfully in containers, and should be grown as a feature plant in pots up a decorative trellis. If you plan to do this check the height of the variety you choose before planting. This can vary from 1½–5ft/46cm–1.5m. If your pots are on an exposed patio or roof garden they may require protection, both from the wind and birds.

Radishes—for the container gardener, the ordinary globe-shaped summer radish is a fine plant to grow in pots alongside lettuces, or it can be used as a filler among containers of brassicas.

Salad greens—these add a lovely peppery flavor to salads and are good to have in containers just outside your kitchen door so they are within easy reach.

Scallions—these are delicious in salads and are great for any containers as they are quick growing and don't take up too much room.

Tomatoes—dwarf tomatoes (plants that grow little more than 8in/20cm high) are very suitable for growing in window boxes and small pots, but the yield is not high. Sow two seeds in a small pot and discard the weaker if they both germinate.

Zucchini—you may need to raise zucchini in pots first, and then plant out when the soil has warmed up, especially in frost-prone areas. Plants grown in pots need to be hardened off by putting them outside during the day (and back under cover at night) before they can be finally planted in position in the container. Grow zucchini in a rich soil mix.

carrot & red pepper booster
serves 2

generous 1 cup carrot juice. generous 1 cup tomato juice. 2 large red bell peppers, seeded and roughly chopped. 1 tbsp lemon juice. freshly ground black pepper

Pour the carrot juice and tomato juice into a food processor and process gently until combined.

Add the red bell peppers and lemon juice. Season with plenty of pepper and process until smooth. Pour the mixture into tall glasses, add straws, and serve immediately.

growing fruit
soft fruit and rhubarb

Many different types of soft fruit can be grown even in a small garden. Cane fruit such as blackberries and raspberries grow vertically, bush fruit like currants or gooseberries take up little space, while strawberry plants may be grown by paths, in pots, or in a barrel.

Strawberries

There are several forms of these popular, easily grown herbaceous fruit, including perpetual and alpine, but the summer-fruiting varieties are most common. Once planted, they are usually left for three or four years before being removed and discarded, with fresh beds prepared for new plants. It is possible to grow summer-fruiting types as an annual crop producing high-quality fruit, but they will not grow as prolifically as well-established two- or three-year-old plants. Plant bare-rooted, summer-fruiting varieties between midsummer and early fall and container-grown plants at any time when the soil is workable. Prepare strawberry beds by digging the soil in late spring or early summer, and adding well-decomposed garden compost or manure. Remove and burn perennial weeds. Just before planting, dust the surface with a general fertilizer. When planting bare-rooted plants, spread out the roots over a small mound of soil at the bottom of the hole, and check that the crown of the plant is level with the surrounding ground. Firm the soil around the roots. With container-grown plants do not bury the

strawberries in barrels

For more than a hundred years strawberries have been grown in wooden barrels with holes cut in their sides. Good drainage is essential. Drill drainage holes in the bottom of the barrel, add clean rubble, and place a 4–6-in/10–15cm-wide wire-netting tube filled with drainage material in the center. Fill the barrel with well-drained soil mix, and put a plant into each hole.

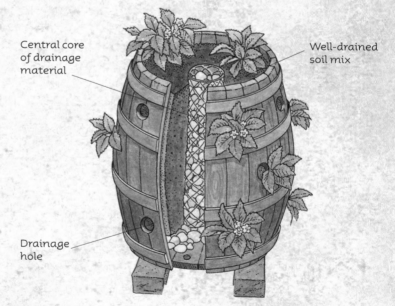

Central core of drainage material

Well-drained soil mix

Drainage hole

Growing strawberries in pots is popular in small gardens. It is a good way of preventing slugs and snails damaging the fruit, although you will still have to watch out for birds!

crown but keep it level with the soil surface. After planting, water the soil thoroughly and pull up weeds regularly.

Blackberries

Blackberries are easy to grow and will thrive in a wide range of sites and soil conditions. Though they prefer sun, they will produce fruit even when grown in deep shade.

Blackberries flower late so frost is not a problem and the fruit grows from late summer through to mid-fall.

Gooseberries

Gooseberries will tolerate partial shade and quite harsh conditions although they prefer full sun. These plants are a good choice for a smaller garden as they produce a lot of fruit for their size.

Blueberries

Blueberries grow in light, free-draining acidic soil with lots of compost dug in. They are ideal for small gardens as the bushes are quite compact and can be easily grown in pots.

Huckleberries

Huckleberries are closely related to blueberries and also like light, free-draining acidic soil with plenty of sun and little shade. The berries are ready for picking from mid- to late summer.

Planting strawberries

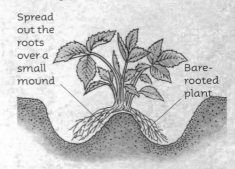

Spread out the roots over a small mound

Bare-rooted plant

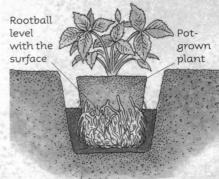

Rootball level with the surface

Pot-grown plant

raspberry trifle

serves 4

2 cups ricotta cheese. ½ cup sugar. 1 tsp vanilla extract. 2 tbsp orange-flower water. 1 tbsp honey.
2 pints raspberries (reserve 1 cup for the topping). 2 pints blueberries (reserve 1 cup for the topping).
1 sponge or pound cake. ¼ cup orange-flower water. Scant ⅓ cup orange juice.
24 ladyfingers. 1 cup heavy cream, whipped.

Mix the ricotta, sugar and vanilla together and set aside.

Combine the 2 tablespoons orange-flower water and honey and toss with the berries. Slice the cake and cut the slices into triangle pieces. Line the bottom of an 8-inch/20-cm springform pan with some of the cake and sprinkle with the ¼ cup of orange-flower water.

Line the sides with the ladyfingers, then spread half of the ricotta mixture over the cake layer. Sprinkle with some of the berries and place another layer of cake down on the top. Sprinkle with the orange juice and spread some ricotta cream and berries over the top. The last layer should be a layer of cake. Cover with whipped cream and decorate with the reserved berries. Chill overnight.

Raspberries

There are two types of raspberry: summer- and fall-fruiting. Established summer-fruiting varieties produce most fruit. Pruning the canes is described on page 39, and picking and storing on page 31.

A tiered framework of wires is essential, using strong posts (up to 12ft/3.6m apart) with galvanized wires strained between them at a height of 2½ft/75cm, 3½ft/1m, and 5¼ft/1.6m above ground. Plant bare-rooted canes during late fall and early winter, or in early spring, spacing them 18in/46cm apart. Immediately after planting, cut all canes to 9–12in/23–30cm high just above a healthy bud.

top tip

Put ⅔ cup frozen raspberries and 1¼ cups sparkling mineral water into a blender and blend until smooth. Briefly blend in 2 scoops of black currant sorbet to make a refreshing crush.

Raspberries are not always red: there are also yellow-gold, purple, and black varieties, but they are always a treat, especially if homegrown!

Planting black currants

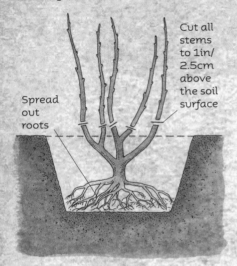

Spread out roots

Cut all stems to 1in/2.5cm above the soil surface

Black currants

These are borne on deciduous bushes for picking during the latter part of midsummer and late summer. Position each plant slightly deeper than usual to allow for soil settlement, and encourage the development of shoots from below. Space plants 5ft/1.5m apart, and cut all stems to about 1in/2.5cm above the surface. Plant young, container-grown bushes at any time of the year when the soil and weather allow. If you plant in summer, wait until the fall and cut out all the old shoots to soil level. Prune fall to spring planting immediately.

Red or white currants

Red currant and white currant bushes are hardy and thrive in open, sunny positions. They

Rhubarb is easy to grow in the kitchen garden, but it is the early, tender, forced stems that have the best flavor.

are tolerant of some shade and can make an attractive feature for a north-facing wall. Bushes will produce 10lb/4.5kg of fruit a year.

Rhubarb

Rhubarb is in a class of its own: it's a vegetable, although it is always cooked like a soft fruit to make pies, compôtes, and jam. Unlike most vegetables rhubarb is a perennial and so can be left in the ground and will return a crop for as many as 10 or even 15 years.

Rhubarb can be grown in an open site on a wide range of soils, as long as they are rich and well-drained. It is also quite hardy and is able to withstand lack of water. Apart from applying a heavy layer of garden compost every fall or spring, rhubarb will survive and produce good yields with little other tending.

growing fruit
harvesting soft fruit

Soft summer fruit is best eaten as soon as possible after it is picked. Care is needed when picking the berries to prevent damage that will limit their life. Always put them into wide-based containers so that there is less chance of you knocking them over.

Bush fruit

Currants—pick these when ripe from mid- to late summer when the weather is dry. Berries can be picked individually but keep better when the entire cluster is removed. They are best eaten at once, but can be stored in a refrigerator for one week.

Gooseberries—pick the fruit from the end of early summer, through midsummer to the early part of late summer, depending on the variety. When fully ripe the berries are soft and fully colored. They can be stored in a refrigerator for a couple of weeks.

Blueberries and huckleberries—pick the fruit when fully ripe from the end of early summer onward depending on your climatic

Gooseberries are a popular soft fruit with a distinctive tart flavor. Pick them individually when they are fully ripe and evenly colored.

safety first

● Care is needed when picking the fruit. Systematically work down rows or around bushes, so that you do not miss ripe fruit. If you do, it will quickly be eaten by wasps.

● Place berries in small, wide-based flat containers that will not be knocked over. When half-full, transfer them into a larger firm-based container and do not put them where children or dogs can knock them over.

● If several varieties are being picked, put them in separate containers so that their flavors can later be compared.

● As soon as possible, move the fruit into a cool room and do not put them near strongly scented vegetables or herbs.

● Where freezing is appropriate, do this as soon as possible.

conditions and location. The fruit may ripen at different times so regular picking may be required. The fruit keeps well in the refrigerator for about a week.

Cane fruit

Raspberries—pick summer-fruiting varieties from the early part of midsummer to late summer, and fall-fruiting types from late summer to mid-fall. The berries are ripe when fully colored yet still firm. Hold the fruit gently and pull, leaving the stalk and plug attached to the plant. Raspberries are best eaten at once, but can be frozen (see below).

Blackberries—pick these when soft and fully ripe by holding each fruit and pulling gently. They are best eaten at once, but can be frozen. Harvest hybrid soft fruit (crosses between a raspberry and a blackberry), such as loganberries and boysen-berries, in the same way.

Other soft fruit

Strawberries—check the crop daily and pick fruit when they are red all over. They are best eaten within a few days.

Rhubarb—the best time is in spring but it can be "forced" for an even earlier crop by covering over the first shoots.

Red currants are an excellent culinary fruit. An established bush will provide 10lb/4.5kg each year.

picking and freezing raspberries

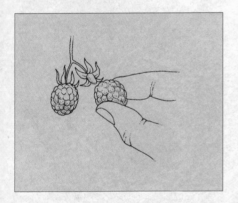

1 Pick the berries individually, when fully colored yet still firm. The plug (the small stalk) should remain on the plant. It is necessary to pick over the plants several times. If left, the fruit soon decays.

2 Freeze raspberries as soon as possible after picking. Select small, underripe berries and space them apart in flat-based plastic containers. Place in the freezer until frozen and then transfer to freezer bags.

picking gooseberries

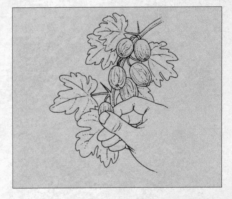

Pick the berries individually, when ripe and fully colored. This varies between varieties—some are early while others are late maturing and ripening. It is necessary to pick over each bush several times.

growing fruit
tree fruit (pome fruit)

Tree fruit fall into two categories: pome fruit and pit fruit. Pome fruit have flesh around a central core which contains the seeds. The apple is one of the best known pome fruits and is one of the easiest tree fruit to grow, even in a small garden. Pears are also popular, although they are a little more demanding.

Planting and growing apples

In the past, apple trees often grew 20ft/6m high or more, and were difficult to prune and harvest. Today, dwarf

Apple trees can be grown in tubs or large pots, but plant only those growing on dwarf rootstocks.

bush apples, cordons, and espaliers are ideal to grow in a small garden. Bushes demand less pruning than cordons, while espaliers require more attention.

Choose a site in full sun that is sheltered from strong winds. Before deciding on an apple tree for your garden check the apple varieties for cold hardiness, disease-resistance, and pollination needs.

Well-drained moisture-retentive soil is essential. Bare-rooted trees are planted during their dormant period in winter. When planting out, mix in plenty of well-rotted garden compost or manure. Cooking apple trees grow well on heavier soils.

Support cordons and espaliers with galvanized wires tensioned between strong posts about 8–12ft/2.4–3.6m apart; space the wires about 15–18in/38–46cm apart to about 7ft/2.1m high. You will need to check the posts every spring for signs of wind damage.

apple trees in tubs

An apple tree in a container is the best way to grow fruit in a small garden. Dwarf rootstocks make this possible, using 15-in/38-cm-wide wooden tubs or pots. Well-drained, moisture-retentive compost is essential and in summer regular watering is needed. During winter it may be necessary to wrap straw around the tub to prevent the roots freezing. Repotting every other late winter is essential, as is feeding during summer. Large crops are not possible with a tub-grown tree but good varieties to seek out include 'Gravenstein', and 'Sundowner'.

Pears grown as cordons or espaliers are best for planting in a small garden. The fruit is easily picked without the need for a stepladder.

Planting and growing pears

The range of rootstocks for pears is limited so that it is not possible to grow pears on trees as small as dwarf apples. Few gardens can accommodate pear trees up to 20ft/6m high, and therefore in small plots it is best to grow pears as cordons or espaliers. Cordon pears planted 2½ft/75cm apart each produce 4–6lb/1.8–2.7kg of fruit a year, while an espalier yields up to 15–25lb/6.8–11.3kg.

The same methods are used for planting and supporting pears as for apples, but pears are more susceptible to drought than apples, so be

prepared to water the soil copiously during dry periods. It is probably better to select a dessert variety than a cooker, but it will need a compatible pollinator that will flower at the same time. 'Conference,' for example, is only partly self-fertile and needs other varieties, such as 'Seckel' or 'Harrow Delight.' Alternatively, if you have a warm garden, plant 'Comice', also 'Highland' (this has the bonus of keeping the fruit from late fall to early winter).

Cordon	Espalier
Single, inclined stem	Tiered branches

Espalier supports

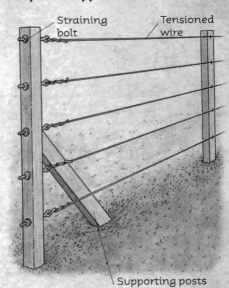

Straining bolt · Tensioned wire · Supporting posts

growing fruit
tree fruit (pit fruit)

The second type of tree fruit are the pit fruit such as peaches, nectarines, plums, and cherries. The juicy flesh surrounds a hard pit containing a kernel. Plums are easily grown whereas peaches, nectarines, and apricots need a warm climate. Cherries, though less tender, are more labor intensive.

Growing peaches and nectarines

In areas where frost is likely in early and mid-spring, the lack of pollinating insects at that time can make it difficult to grow peaches and nectarines successfully. Where conditions are least favorable, choose a peach over a nectarine, and always grow it as a fan trained on galvanized wires against a warm, sunny, south- or southwest-facing wall rather than as a bush.

Construct tiers of galvanized wires before planting a peach or nectarine. Position the lowest wire 1ft/30cm above the ground, with others 8in/20cm apart to a height of about 6ft/1.8m. Secure the wires 4in/10cm from the wall. Because peaches and nectarines are best grown against a wall it is essential to thoroughly prepare the soil by adding plenty of moisture-retentive, well-decayed garden compost or manure. Prepare an area 18in/46cm deep and 3½ft/1m square and position the main stem about 9in/23cm from the wall. Plant bare-rooted specimens in late fall or early winter, and container-grown plants at any time when the soil and weather allow. Choose a two- or three-year-old plant with eight or more branches.

top tip

To make a yummy nectarine melt, gradually blend scant 1 cup milk with 12oz/350g lemon sorbet until combined. Then add 1 ripe mango and 2 ripe nectarines, all peeled, pitted, and diced, and process until smooth.

A reliable variety of peach includes 'Elegant Lady.' Both peaches and nectarines are self-fertile and begin to fruit within about three or four years.

Secure the stems to bamboo canes, and then to the wires. The two main arms should be at an upward 45° angle, with other stems spaced out.

Growing plums

These are popular tree fruit. Because they flower early in the year and are vulnerable to frost, plant them in a mild area. Plums can be grown in several forms, including standards, half-standards, bushes, and pyramids, but in small gardens a fan-trained form is better.

Prepare the soil in the same way as for peaches, and with a similar arrangement of tiered wires against a wall. Plant and prune fan-trained plants in the same way.

Growing apricots

Apricot trees like a sunny site but can tolerate a wide range of soils. Trees are self-fertile,

hand pollinating

Peaches and nectarines flower early in the year when pollinating insects are scarce. Therefore, use a soft brush or loose ball of cotton wool to gently dab each flower every other day from the time the buds open until the petals fall.

but tend to produce more successfully if planted near other varieties. They begin producing fruit when they are three or four years old.

Growing cherries

Cherry trees need an open site in full sun and rich soil. Sweet cherry (Prunus avium) is not self-fertile so you need at least two. Semidwarf varieties are suitable for small gardens.

Fan trained

Plum trees flower early in the season and therefore need a warm, sheltered position, ideally against a wall. This is an ideal form for small gardens.

growing fruit
harvesting and storing tree fruit

The many types of tree fruit all have a different nature, both with their picking and storage qualities. It is important to know the correct way to harvest tree fruit in order to extend its keeping qualities. The periods when the fruit is ready to be picked also vary.

Picking tree fruit

Careful picking is essential. Fruit that is roughly handled becomes bruised and does not last long when stored.

Apples—these vary in their picking time from midsummer to mid-fall. Their storage period is also variable: some varieties need to be eaten within a few weeks whereas others may last into the following spring.

Pick apples when the stalk readily parts from the tree.

Test each fruit by cupping it in the palm of your hand and gently raising and turning it. If the stalk parts from the tree it is ready for picking.

Store the apples by placing them slightly apart in slatted trays in a cool, airy, vermin- and frost-proof shed. If the air is dry, wrap them in oiled paper and place them folded side down. Also, regularly check the apples to make sure they are not starting to decay.

Alternatively, place 4lb/1.8kg of the same variety of apples in a plastic bag punctured with holes. Fold over the top and store as above.

Pears—these have a shorter storage life than apples and the picking time is harder to judge. Some varieties are ready in late summer, others in mid-fall. Judging when a fruit is ready to be picked is

the same as for apples. Because early varieties, if left on the tree, become mealy and soft, pick them before they are completely ready by using scissors to sever the stalks. Store in a cool, dry, airy, dark, vermin-proof shed. Place pears individually in slatted trays, leaving space between them. Alternatively, you can wrap them but this prevents you seeing the onset of decay.

Peaches and nectarines—pick the fruit when the skin reveals a reddish flush and the flesh around the stalk softens. This happens from the latter part of midsummer to fall.

Pick by holding a fruit in the palm of your hand and gently lifting and twisting; it is ready when the stalk separates easily. The fruit is best eaten fresh, but can be stored in a cool place for about a week.

top tip

For a classic filling for pies, peel, core, and chop 2lb/900g cooking apples and mix together in a bowl along with 2 ½ cups blackberries, ¼ cup light brown sugar, and 1 tsp ground cinnamon.

storing pears

  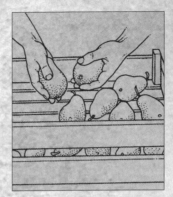 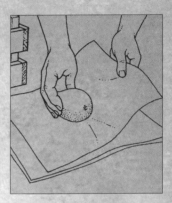

1 Supporting the pear in your palm, lift and twist the fruit very gently. If the stalk readily parts from the tree, the fruit is ready to be picked.

2 Early varieties can be picked before they are completely ready by using scissors. If left too long on the tree they become soft and mealy.

3 Store pears on slatted trays. Space the fruit apart, so that they do not touch. This reduces the risk of decaying fruit contaminating others.

4 Usually, pears can be left unwrapped, but in a dry atmosphere wrap them individually. However, this does mask the early signs of decay.

Plums—pick fruit from the latter part of midsummer to late fall, when it parts from the tree leaving the stalk behind. Store plums in slatted boxes lined with tissue paper. Check them daily for decay.

Apricots—harvest before the fruit has fully ripened on the tree. The fruit is ready when it has attained a uniform color and the skin gives slightly when pressed.

Cherries—bird damage will tell you when your fruit is ripe! Cherries are best eaten soon after picking because they bruise easily and then spoil.

Cherries are delicious but you must pick them quickly otherwise the birds will get there before you.

growing fruit
pruning bush, cane, and tree fruit

Bush, cane, and tree fruit differ in the way they produce fruit. Some develop fruit on young, newly produced shoots, others on an existing framework. Therefore, pruning must be carried out to encourage the development of suitable shoots, as well as to allow light and air to reach the plants.

Bush fruit

These are popular choices for small gardens as they take up little space and produce fruit within a few years of being planted.

Black currants—on planting, cut all stems to one or two buds above the soil. During the following year, new stems develop, which are left to grow and bear fruit. Between late fall and early spring the following year, and thereafter, prune by cutting to ground level all the shoots that produced fruit. Also, cut out thin, weak, and diseased shoots to allow light and air to enter the bush.

Gooseberries—established bushes have a permanent framework upon which short, fruit-bearing spurs develop. Newly planted gooseberry bushes without a framework of branches should be pruned in winter by cutting back all shoots by half. Prune established bushes in winter; cut out diseased, damaged,

Blackberries are tolerant of most soils and can even grow in the deepest shade. Once established, blackberries require little care.

Pruning gooseberries

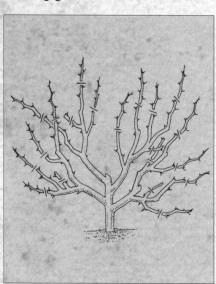

Raspberries and other cane fruit need annual pruning to encourage the growth of young canes that will bear fruit during the following year.

Pruning raspberries

Summer fruiting

Fall fruiting

and overcrowded shoots. Also, cut back by half all the shoots produced during the previous season, and reduce the side-shoots to about 2in/5cm long.

Red currants and white currants—these are pruned like gooseberries.

Cane fruit

Being upright these will fit into narrow positions, perhaps alongside a path.

Summer-fruiting raspberries —they fruit on upright canes produced the previous year. Prune established plants in the fall by cutting out all canes that produced fruit in the summer. Leave the young canes tied to supporting wires to fruit the following year.

Fall-fruiting raspberries— they fruit on canes produced earlier the same year. Prune established plants in late winter and cut all canes to ground level. In spring, as the canes grow, cut out weak ones and tie the remaining ones to supporting wires.

Blackberries and hybrid berries—they fruit on canes produced the previous year. Immediately after picking the berries, cut down to the base all canes that produced fruit. Then spread out the remaining young canes and tie them to supporting wires.

top tip For a quick and delicious dessert, sandwich together two homemade shortcake cookies with freshly whipped cream and raspberries.

Tree fruit

It usually takes several years before a good framework of branches and fruiting spurs is formed. Where space is limited, plant cordon, espalier, and fan-trained forms against a wall, or secure them to a framework of tiered wires.

Apples and pears—during the first four years it is essential to develop healthy, well-positioned branches. Once they are established, pruning creates a balance between maintaining and renewing the framework and retaining a proportion of the existing fruiting wood and spurs, while developing others. Creating and maintaining this framework is a task best tackled in winter. However, when apples and pears are grown as cordons and espaliers, pruning will also be needed during the summer to retain the shape and inhibit the growth of unnecessary shoots. Do not be in a hurry for the tree to bear fruit.

Plums—these are usually grown as bushes or fans. When creating a framework of branches in a young tree, prune in mid-spring, just as the sap is rising. Try to create three to five strong branches. Later, prune in early summer,

It's important to prune plum trees annually to encourage strong, vigorous, and productive growth, and large fruit. Pruning also helps keep pests and diseases under control.

removing all dead and diseased wood to keep the tree healthy and not congested. With fan-trained trees, prune in spring to create short side-shoots that grow from the framework.

Peaches and nectarines—always prune in late winter or early spring, when growth begins, but never tackle this task in winter. Initially, the purpose of pruning is to encourage the development of a fan. Pruning a two- or three-year-old plant is much easier than creating a fan from a rooted shoot with no side-shoots. On an established plant, cut back each arm of the fan by about one third, making cuts slightly above a downward pointing bud. In the following summer, shoots develop on each arm; allow three to form and tie each of them to a cane.

cherry pie

serves 4

1 lb 2oz/500 g prepared pie dough. Butter for greasing. Water, for sealing. 1 beaten egg, for glazing. 2 lb/900 g pitted fresh cherries. 1/2 tsp almond extract. 1/4 tsp allspice. 3/4 cup sugar. 2 tbsp cornstarch. 2 tbsp water.

Preheat the oven to 425°F/220°C. Grease a 9-inch/23-cm round pie-dish with butter. Roll out the dough into 2 circles, each 12 in/30 cm in diameter. Use one to line the pie dish. Trim, leaving an overhang of 1/2 in/1 cm.

Place half the cherries and the sugar in a large pan. Bring to a simmer over a low heat, stirring, until the sugar has melted. Stir in the almond extract and allspice.

In a separate bowl, mix the cornstarch and water to form a paste. Remove the pan from the heat, stir in the cornstarch, then return to the heat and stir constantly until the mixture boils and thickens. Let cool a little. Stir in the remaining cherries, pour into the pastry shell, then dot with butter.

Use the other dough circle to cover the pie. Trim the edge, seal with water, then brush with beaten egg. Make two slits in the center to let out the steam. Cover with foil, then bake for 30 minutes. Remove from the oven, discard the foil, then bake for 15 minutes, or until golden.

Also, use a thumb to rub out buds growing toward the wall. During late summer, when each of these shoots is 18in/46cm long, nip out their growing points.

Apricots—young trees should be trained to have an open center (leader trunk removed), with many well-spaced branches that are capable of bearing their heavy fruit without breaking. Shoots and suckers should be pruned annually to encourage the growth of fruiting spurs.

Cherries—a young tree, like apricots, should be trained to have an open center encircled by well-spaced branches. Prune in late winter to encourage growth the following year. Only prune in summer when the tree has reached the desired size.

If you have fruit trees in the garden you will not be short of recipe ideas for late summer and fall, and what could be better than a basket of your own produce?

care and maintenance
protecting kitchen garden crops

Cloches and polytunnels are useful in almost every season in the kitchen garden, but never more so than when bad weather is threatening to damage crops. They keep off rain, wind, and a degree of frost where that occurs and can protect plants from attack by some pests. In late winter and early spring they give early plants extra protection, which will bring them on well ahead of the rest. Earlier still, they can be used to cover strips of soil required for early sowing. Keeping the rain off the soil will allow it to warm up and become workable much earlier than uncovered areas.

Tunnels and cloches are most suitable for low-growing plants, though with imagination they can also be pressed into service for taller crops. A pair of barn cloches, stood on end and wired together, are perfect around outdoor tomato plants to ripen the last fruit in the fall.

Cloches

Cloches are made from glass or rigid plastic. Glass has the advantage of retaining heat better and being more stable in windy weather, but it is very fragile and dangerous when broken, especially in gardens where children play. It is also expensive, and makes cloches heavy and awkward to move about. Plastic cloches are cheap and lightweight, and not as easily broken as glass; they do not retain so much warmth and need to be thoroughly

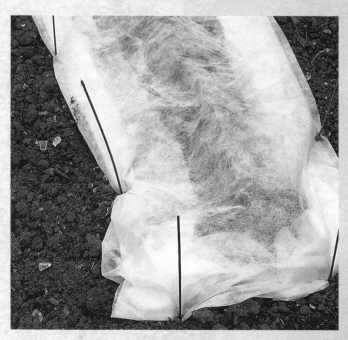

The earliest cloches were used for individual plants. Bell-type cloches are still available, but open-ended styles are now more popular.

A lightweight horticultural blanket made from polypropylene provides young plants with surprisingly good protection against adverse weather.

The polytunnel is very popular with gardeners because it is cheap to buy and easy to use. However, it does have a relatively short life.

secured or they will blow away in even slightly windy weather. Cloches may be made from clear plastic, PVC, twin-walled polycarbonate, or polypropylene. All plastic should have been treated with an ultraviolet inhibitor.

Early cloches were bell-shaped (cloche is French for bell) or lantern-shaped, and used to cover individual plants. This type of cloche is still available but larger cloches, used end-to-end to cover whole rows of plants, are now more popular. They may be made from two pieces of glass (or plastic) fixed together in an inverted "V" to form a tent shape, or from four pieces of glass to form a barn cloche with its slightly sloping sides topped by a wide tent roof. The barn cloche is useful for taller plants, and can usually be ventilated by raising or removing one side of the roof. Another popular cloche shape is an arc, made by bending a flexible, semirigid sheet of plastic, usually corrugated, and securing it with hoops.

To prevent rows of cloches from becoming wind tunnels, they should be fitted with end panels, which sometimes have adjustable ventilators. Cloches with built-in sprinklers are also available for easy watering.

Polytunnels

These are made from plastic sheeting that is stretched over wire hoops positioned over the crop. They are usually available as packs of hoops with a separate plastic sheet, but brands that have the plastic ready-fitted over the hoops and which are folded up, concertina fashion, make erecting the tunnels easier. They are cheap, and easy to use and store.

Floating row cover

This is a term applied to lightweight perforated plastic or fiber materials that lie loosely on top of the crop, and are held in place by the edges being buried or staked in the ground. The material is light and flexible enough not to restrict the crop as it grows. Polypropylene fiber fleece is the most popular, and insulates the plants against cold and wind while remaining permeable to air and moisture. It tears easily but with care will last for several seasons, especially if it has strengthened edges.

care and maintenance
pollination

Plants reproduce sexually by means of seed. The seeds need to be dispersed as widely as possible, but the plant is at a disadvantage because it is rooted to one spot. Animals and birds, however, can move about freely; one of the main ways plants disperse their seed is by encouraging an animal or bird to carry it away. Embedding the seed within a sweet, juicy, edible fruit will certainly attract a range of creatures to help distribute the seed as far and wide as possible.

The process of bearing fruit is therefore usually inextricably linked with sexual reproduction and the formation of seed. In order to form seed, pollen grains from the male part of a flower must be transferred to the stigma that is attached to the ovary, the female part of a flower—the process known as pollination.

Pollination is followed by fertilization when the male and female cells fuse to produce an embryo, or seed, which swells to form a fruit. If pollination and fertilization do not occur, the fruit generally (though not always) fails to form. When we grow fruit trees and bushes in our gardens, therefore, we need to make sure that pollination and fertilization of the flowers can take place.

Cross-pollination and self-pollination

Many flowers achieve pollination very easily, without the need for any outside help. Although there can be separate male and female flowers (sometimes on the same plant or sometimes on separate plants), most species bear flowers containing both male and female sexual organs. Sometimes pollen can fertilize the female cells of the same flower (self-pollination), but often the flowers are "self-incompatible." This means that the pollen needs to come from a different flower, or a different plant or variety of the same species (cross-pollination).

Many tree fruits need to be cross-pollinated to bear a good crop of fruit. Some varieties are partially self-fertile so that a small crop will be carried even if no other fruit trees are nearby, but the crop will be greatly increased by cross-

Apple blossom must be pollinated before a crop can be carried. It is usually necessary to grow at least two compatible varieties.

pollination. Because flying insects are responsible for pollination, trees must be within flight distance of suitable partners.

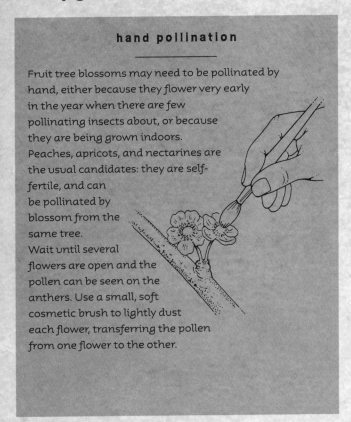

hand pollination

Fruit tree blossoms may need to be pollinated by hand, either because they flower very early in the year when there are few pollinating insects about, or because they are being grown indoors. Peaches, apricots, and nectarines are the usual candidates: they are self-fertile, and can be pollinated by blossom from the same tree. Wait until several flowers are open and the pollen can be seen on the anthers. Use a small, soft cosmetic brush to lightly dust each flower, transferring the pollen from one flower to the other.

Pollinating partners

The two varieties of tree grown as partners must be compatible, and flower at the same time. There are a few incompatible varieties: for example, 'Cox's Orange Pippin' will not pollinate, or be pollinated by, 'Kidd's Orange Red.' Fruit catalogs have information on flowering times, dividing them into early, mid-season, and late, usually indicating this by numbers 1, 2, and 3. Choose two varieties from the same pollinating group—for instance, 'William's Pride' and 'Chehalis.' Varieties from adjoining groups usually have sufficient overlap to be successful, but a Group 1 variety will not pollinate a Group 3.

Looking after insect pollinators

Bees and other nectar-seeking insects are very efficient pollinators of tree fruit. It's really important, therefore, to make sure that you never spray the trees with insecticide during the flowering season.

top tip A local nursery or garden society may be able to tell you which native plants to grow to attract bees to your garden. Aim to have a steady supply of plants in bloom to extend the period during which bees will be gathering nectar and so pollinating your fruit trees.

Pear blossom: pear trees need to be cross-pollinated in order to produce a decent-sized crop of fruit.

growing herbs
herb garden design

Several herbs, such as the biennial angelica, are large and dominant—and best planted in herbaceous or large herb borders. Most herbs though, are suitable for small gardens, while prostrate varieties can be easily planted between paving slabs arranged in a checkerboard pattern.

top tip

Liven up potato wedges by adding

1 tbsp chopped fresh rosemary,

1 tbsp chopped fresh parsley, and

1 tbsp chopped fresh thyme to a

little melted butter and oil, and

chopped garlic. Coat the parboiled

wedges in the mixture and cook in

a skillet for 10–15 minutes.

The garden design

A well-structured herb garden is a highly ornamental feature in its own right, capable of occupying a defined part of a large garden, or—planned with care—of making an appealing garden in itself. Traditionally, herb gardens have been planned in the same way as rose gardens with small plots arranged within a formal, geometric structure, each bed enclosed by a low hedge of clipped box. The geometry and formality can be complemented by the use of gravel, brick, or stone paving for paths and the whole is intricately ornamental. Herbs growing in beds without an enclosure can spill out onto the hard surface for a more informal look, and they also take very well to being planted in containers. Either of these treatments can work well for a patio garden.

While a symmetrical plan based on mirrored beds within a square or rectangle can look overdesigned in a smaller garden, the formality of straight-edged planting areas, evergreen edging, and hard surfaces can be adapted in many ways to produce a garden with a true herbarium appeal but without the overdemanding symmetry. The materials used

A herb wheel, closely planted with segments of contrasting thymes, creates an attractive feature that is easy to manage.

Cobbles set in concrete surrounding a small water feature are a strong design focus of this formally laid-out herb garden.

for the hard-landscaping of the garden should be in sympathy with the house.

A highly formalized herb garden with clipped hedging needs to be kept manicured to look at its best. An informal style can benefit from a slightly neglected look. However you decide to design your garden, remember that you will need to reach the plants for harvesting.

Cartwheel herb gardens

These are ornamental and functional features that can be tailored to fit areas only 6ft/1.8m square. If possible, use an old cartwheel, but a simulated design is easily created by using large pebbles to mark out the circumference and spokes.

Checkerboard designs

This is a novel way to grow low-growing herbs. Select an area, perhaps 7½ft/2.28m square, which drains freely but is not too dry. Then lay 18in-/46cm-square paving slabs in a checkerboard arrangement leaving alternate squares uncovered. Plant the uncovered squares with low-growing herbs. Where herbs do not completely cover the soil, spread pea gravel over the soil. This will look attractive and has the added advantage of reducing moisture loss.

herbs in containers

Small herbs are ideal in window boxes. A variety of low-growing herbs can also be grown in troughs and arranged along the edge of a patio, veranda, or balcony. Troughs and other containers are an excellent way to grow exceptionally invasive herbs, such as mint.

Ornate planters, with cup-shaped holes in their sides, take up very little space. Placed in a sunny position in the garden these planters can be filled with summer herbs, including chives, sorrel, and basil.

Growing bags can be reused with a little general fertilizer. They are excellent for short-lived herbs such as parsley or cilantro.

growing herbs
ornamental herbs

As well as being useful for culinary purposes, there are many herbs that form beautiful and ornamental plants to grace any garden. Some were once grown for their usefulness in medicine, but are now known best as garden flowers and shrubs.

flowering herbs for use and ornament

Angelica—ANGELICA ARCHANGELICA: the stems can be crystallized and the leaves cooked with fish

Borage—BORAGO OFFICINALIS: both young leaves and the brilliant blue flowers are edible

Chamomile—CHAMAEMELUM NOBILE: apple-scented leaves for pot pourri, white flowers for soothing tisanes

Comfrey—SYMPHYTUM OFFICINALE: a tall, leafy plant with purple-blue flowers, which makes excellent garden fertilizer

Feverfew—TANACETUM PARTHENIUM: leaves eaten in sandwiches may help against migraine, flowers deter moths

Lavender—LAVANDULA: purple, scented flowers that can be used in cooking and as a relaxant

Lemon balm—MELISSA OFFICINALIS: leaves and flowers can be made into a soothing tisane

Nasturtium—TROPAEOLUM: velvety, spurred flowers yield green knobby fruits that can be pickled; flowers and peppery leaves are also edible

Growing herbs together

Herbs are used both to flavor food and as medicine, often both at the same time, and they can also be used in a variety of other traditional ways. They offer a good range of colors, scents, and textures and a herbarium, as the herb garden was once called, is a place to delight the senses.

Many herbal plants come from the broad family known as the labiates and their lipped flowers are a magnet to bees so that the garden hums in summer. If you have an interest in history or folklore you may well be lured by the charms of a herb garden and will find yourself making pot pourri and herbal oils and vinegars as well as using the leaves or flowers in cooking and for herbal teas.

Rosemary traditionally accompanies lamb and many Mediterranean dishes.

Although there are herbs for a variety of situations and soils many herbs are of Mediterranean origin and need well-drained soil with

full sun and shelter. Some cultivars with unusual golden or variegated coloring, such as gold-leaf forms of sage or lemon balm, can thrive in light shade. Many aromatics prefer soil that is not too fertile.

Flowers for herb gardens

If you include flowers such as lilies, foxgloves, and roses in your herb garden you will be continuing an old apothecary-garden tradition as well as enlivening the garden with spires and mounds of alluring flowers. Selecting widely, you will be able to achieve great variety using only those plants once grown for their medicinal use. While it is not advisable to use any of the more powerful plants from the old herbals for self-treatment, growing them to look at is another matter.

As well as the flavoring herbs with which we're still familiar, herbs less widely known, some for kitchen use and some with ancient domestic benefits such as pennyroyal—a mint, for keeping fleas at bay—can still be bought from specialist growers. Look out for tansy, rue, bergamot, and sweet cicely and add these to the well-known classics such as chamomile, mint, thyme, and lavender.

Nasturtiums have brightly colored flowers that are a delight in salads.

Profile plants

ROSMARINUS OFFICINALIS
Rosemary
Rosemary makes a lovely shrub with evergreen needles and small light blue flowers that appear from late fall until early summer.
HT AND SP to 5ft/1.5m but can be cut back.
SOIL AND SITUATION Well-drained soil that is not too rich and a sheltered position in full sun.

TROPAEOLUM
Nasturtium
Nasturtiums bring vivid color to the herb garden. The bushy and climbing varieties are easily grown from seed.
HT 12in/30cm (bush)
3–10ft/1–3m (climbing)
SP 18in/46cm (bush)
4ft/1.2m (climbing)

Bees love sage flowers, and the leaves add flavor to stuffing.

SOIL AND SITUATION Well-drained soil that is not too rich in a sunny position.

SALVIA OFFICINALIS
Sage
Sage has lovely purple-blue flowers as well as attractive, gray-green leaves. Golden-leaved (named 'Aurea') and purple-leaved ('Purpurascens') varieties are also available.
HT 30in/75cm
SP 3ft/90cm
SOIL AND SITUATION Fairly fertile, light, and well-drained soil, in a sunny position.

top tip

Sage butter is a tasty addition to a fresh pasta dish. Simply melt 4 tbsp butter in a small saucepan over gentle heat then add 1 bunch of fresh sage leaves, finely chopped.

growing herbs
culinary herbs

Herbs include annuals such as basil that die at the end of summer and perennials such as lemon balm, fennel, and tarragon that die back in winter but grow up again each spring. A few shrubby herbs such as bay, rosemary, and thyme flourish during the winter and are available fresh at any time.

minted fennel salad
serves 4

1 fennel bulb. lemon juice. 2 small oranges. 1 small or ½ large cucumber. 1 tbsp chopped fresh mint. 1 tbsp virgin olive oil. 2 eggs, hard boiled

Using a sharp knife, trim the outer leaves from the fennel. Slice the fennel bulb thinly into a bowl of water and sprinkle with lemon juice.

Using a sharp knife, pare away the orange peel, then segment the oranges by carefully slicing between each line of pith. Do this over the bowl in order to retain the juice.

Using a sharp knife, cut the cucumber into ½-in/1-cm circles and then cut each circle into quarters.

Add the cucumber to the fennel and orange mixture together with the mint.

Pour over the olive oil and toss well. Serve topped with the hard-boiled eggs, cut into quarters.

Nine popular herbs
Caraway—biennial with fern-like leaves and umbrellalike heads of green flowers.
Chives—bulbous, with tubular leaves and rose-pink flowers.
Dill—hardy annual with feathery green leaves and umbrellalike heads of yellow flowers.

Fennel—herbaceous perennial with blue-green leaves and golden-yellow flowers in umbrellalike heads.
Lemon balm—herbaceous perennial with lemon-scented green leaves.

Herbs are essential in a kitchen garden for adding flavor to a huge range of sweet and savory dishes.

top tip
Chives add a lovely flavor to a batch of homemade cheese scones.

Mint—herbaceous invasive perennial. A wide range, from spearmint to apple mint.

Parsley—biennial, with crinkled or flat (more strongly flavored) green leaves.

Sage—short-lived shrub, with gray-green leaves and spires of violet-blue flowers in early summer. There are forms with more ornamental leaves (purple, and some variegated) that are mainly used to create color in borders.

Thyme—low-growing perennial. Garden thyme is a superb culinary herb, but there are varieties with golden or variegated leaves that are used to add color to checkerboard designs.

rosemary and garlic balsamic vinegar

10 2-inch sprigs rosemary. 4 cloves garlic. 1 cup balsamic vinegar

Wash the rosemary sprigs, dry, and tear off the leaves from the stems. Split the garlic cloves in half lengthwise. Combine the leaves and garlic halves in a clean jar. In a saucepan over medium heat, heat the balsamic vinegar until it just starts to bubble around the edges of the pan. Wait until it cools a little, then pour into the jar with rosemary and garlic. When it is completely cool, cover the jar and store in a cool, dark place. Check occasionally to see whether the vinegar has reached the desired strength.

Before using, strain the vinegar through a fine sieve or cheesecloth into clean jars. Add a fresh sprig of rosemary for decoration and again cover and store in a cool, dark place.

top tip

To make mint-flavored oil, pound mint leaves. Add scant 1 cup of extra virgin olive oil (a little at a time). Pour into a glass bottle and seal tightly. Turn the bottle upside down once every two days. After two weeks it will be ready to serve.

using herbs in the kitchen

ANNUAL AND SHORT-LIVED HERBS

Basil—OCIMUM BASILICUM: spicily aromatic, used in pesto and salads; has an affinity with tomatoes

Cilantro—CORIANDRUM SATIVUM: the leaves have a spicy, lemony flavor much used in Asian cuisine

Dill—ANETHUM GRAVEOLENS: cool, aromatic flavor that marries well with potato salad and fish

Garlic—ALLIUM SATIVUM: these are strongly piquant bulb plants that are often classed as a herb because of their usefulness in providing flavor in cooking; they give dishes a Mediterranean flavor

Parsley—PETROSELINUM CRISPUM: indispensable garnishing herb

PERENNIAL AND SHRUBBY HERBS

Bay—LAURUS NOBILIS: leathery evergreen leaves for bouquet garni (bay can be grown as topiary)

Chives—ALLIUM SCHOENOPRASUM: onion-flavored leaves for garnishes

Fennel—FOENICULUM VULGARE: feathery leaves have a slightly anise taste

French tarragon—ARTEMISIA DRANUNCULUS: a subtle anise flavor for chicken and sauces

Marjoram—ORIGANUM VULGARE: a good herb for soups, stews, and bouquet garni; also for pizza

Winter Savory—SATUREJA MONTANA: the pungent leaves are good for use in salt-free diets

Mint—MENTHA SPICATA: also known as spearmint, a well-known cooling and refreshing herb for mint sauce, new potatoes, and peas. Pineapple mint (M. SUAVEOLENS 'VARIEGATA') and eau-de-cologne mint (M. X PIPERATA F. CITRATA, syn. M. CITRATA) are two of the more unusual varieties

Rosemary—ROSMARINUS OFFICINALIS: aromatic needles go well with lamb; also for pot pourri and cosmetic uses

Sage—SALVIA OFFICINALIS: for pork dishes and sage and onion stuffing

Salad burnet—POTERIUM SANSQUISORBA: cucumber-flavored leaves for salads and summer drinks

Thyme—THYMUS VULGARIS: aromatic shrubby herb for bouquet garni and for adding to soups and stews

SEASONAL GARDENING

spring
early spring: general tasks

This is the time to use up some of those crops that have remained all winter in the vegetable plot, and to start preparing for the new season's harvest. With a little careful planning, it's possible to enjoy fresh produce from the kitchen garden at almost any time of the year.

Harvest rhubarb

Not everyone considers rhubarb to be a gourmet treat but the tender forced stems are a real delicacy at this time of year, far removed from the tough, acid, stringy stalks at the end of the season.

The earliest crops of rhubarb are obtained by boxing up roots and forcing them into growth in a greenhouse, but plants can also be forced outdoors, covering the crowns in situ with purpose-made forcing pots or black plastic trash cans to exclude all light.

Those covered up in early or midwinter will probably have shoots ready for harvesting now, depending on how mild the weather has been in the preceding weeks.

Protect blossom on early-flowering fruit trees

In cold districts frosts remain a possibility in early spring, and will kill the blossoms on some of the early-flowering fruit trees such as apricots and peaches, often ruining the chance of a good crop. Protect the trees from night chill by draping them with a lightweight polypropylene fleece or, if the trees are growing against a wall or fence, attach a roll-down screen of fine-mesh netting.

When fruit trees flower early in the year, while the weather is still cold, it is well worth pollinating the blossom yourself using a small, soft cosmetic brush to transfer pollen gently among the flowers (see page 45).

use up overwintered crops

Parsnips that have remained in the kitchen garden all winter are ready for digging up and using as required. Now that spring has arrived, the roots will soon begin to grow again, signaled by small green tufts emerging from the tops of the plants. As growth continues, the roots will become soft and flabby so should be harvested now. Leeks will also start into growth again, producing flower buds that develop in their second year. This results in a solid flower stem in the center of the leek that spoils the taste and quality. Any leeks and parsnips remaining should be lifted now and moved to a spare piece of ground until used up.

top tip

Rhubarb and orange are a great combination so try mixing 2lb/ 900g rhubarb, cut into 1-in/ 2.5-cm lengths, with ½ cup superfine sugar and the grated rind and juice of 1 orange. Place in an ovenproof dish and then add your favorite topping.

A purpose-built framework to support a polypropylene fleece will make it easier to protect the early blossoms of fruit trees from a sudden drop in temperature.

rhubarb crisp

serves 4

⅓ cup margarine, softened, plus extra for greasing. 3 cups chopped rhubarb. 1 cup white sugar. ¾ cup rolled oats. 1 tsp all-purpose flour. 1 tsp ground cinnamon. ¾ cup brown sugar. ¾ cup all-purpose flour. ½ tsp baking soda. ½ tsp salt. Whipped cream or vanilla ice cream, to serve

Preheat the oven to 350°F/180°C and lightly grease a 2-quart baking dish.

Put the rhubarb, sugar, oats, 1 teaspoon flour, the cinnamon, and brown sugar in a large bowl and stir until well combined. Pour the mixture into the prepared baking dish.

In a small bowl, stir together ¾ cup of flour, the baking soda, and salt. Blend in the margarine until all the flour is incorporated and sprinkle over the rhubarb mixture.

Bake in the preheated oven for about 30 minutes, or until the rhubarb is tender.

Serve warm with freshly whipped cream or ice cream.

stake peas and beans

The peas and beans that were sown in the fall or early spring should be provided with supports as they grow. For peas you can use plastic netting, supported by stakes at regular intervals; the plants will twine their tendrils around the netting as they grow. Alternatively, a forest of twiggy brushwood sticks provides excellent support if you have a ready supply. Beans will also be happy with twiggy sticks, or you can provide them with a series of stakes along each side of the row, with string running around them to prevent the plants from flopping outward and spoiling.

spring
early spring: sowing and planting

It is time for most gardeners to start sowing in earnest at last, although gardeners with heavy soil or gardens in particularly cold, exposed positions may be better advised to wait a little while longer. Always garden according to the prevailing conditions rather than calendar dates.

Prepare the soil for sowing

Soil in a seedbed should be broken down to fine, even crumbs, usually known as a fine "tilth." If the soil is left in large clods it is very difficult to get a level seedbed, and seeds will end up being buried either too deep or too shallow to achieve good germination.

If the kitchen garden has been left roughly dug over the winter, frosts may have begun to break up the clods of soil, by the action of repeated freezing and thawing.

As soon as some dry, breezy weather has dried out the soil, these clods can be reduced to fine crumbs by raking.

begin sowing vegetable crops

Some time during early spring, depending on the weather, a wide range of vegetables can be sown, including beans, carrots, leeks, lettuces, parsnips, summer and fall cabbages, early summer cauliflowers, spinach, and Swiss chard. Sow the seeds thinly into drills then rake the soil carefully over the seeds, tamp it down lightly, and label the row. It is far too early for tender crops such as zucchini, marrows, pumpkins, squashes, and beans to be sown outside, but they can be raised in pots in a greenhouse for planting out later.

A light touch with the rake is necessary in order to produce a fine, even surface to a seedbed. Large stones should be removed.

plant potatoes

If space is limited, plant early potatoes rather than maincrop, choosing some of the varieties that are hard to buy. The earliest crops of new potatoes have a lovely flavor when they are freshly lifted. The foliage of potatoes is sensitive to frost, so time the planting carefully if you are in a frost-prone area. It generally takes two or three weeks before the shoots show through the soil after planting.

1 As an alternative to immediate planting, seed potatoes can be set on a cool, light windowsill to produce chits (below). The eyes that produce these shoots are clustered together at one end of the tuber, and should be set in egg boxes with this end upward.

3 Draw wide drills using a draw hoe, or use a trowel to make individual planting holes. Plant the potatoes around 5in/13cm deep. Chitted tubers should be dropped carefully into the holes with the shoots at the top; these shoots are very fragile and are easily broken. Unsprouted tubers should be planted with the rose end facing up.

4 Check the rows of potatoes regularly for the first shoots; they are dark bluish-green (right).

Early spring is a good time to plant container-grown cane and bush soft fruit, such as raspberries and black currants.

2 Potatoes should be planted in well-prepared soil in rows 18in/46cm apart, and spaced 12–18in/30–46cm apart within the row (below). The chitted tubers will appear through the soil more quickly after planting, but they need to be handled carefully.

spring
mid-spring: sowing and planting

Time vegetable sowings so that you have a steady harvest throughout the summer, without a glut of crops maturing simultaneously. Be particularly careful with vegetables that have a short period of use before they spoil, such as lettuces, which run to seed, and peas, which become tough.

Continue sowing vegetables

As the weather becomes warmer, more and more vegetable crops can be sown. Among those that can be sown outdoors directly where they are to grow are beet, Swiss chard, various beans, carrots, kohlrabi, lettuce, peas, radishes, scallions, spinach, and turnips. Some vegetables can be sown now in a seedbed and transplanted to their cropping positions later in the year. These include broccoli, Brussels sprouts, calabrese, cauliflowers, cabbages, pumpkins, squashes, and leeks.

sow crops for succession

"Little and often" is a good idea when it comes to sowing many vegetables. This ensures that crops can be picked and used when they are young and tender, and there will be an ongoing supply to follow from later sowings. Crops that can be grown in succession include beet, cabbage, carrots, cauliflower, lettuce, radishes, spinach, and peas. Sow short rows at two- to four-week intervals, or select a range of varieties to mature at different times.

Try to keep the kitchen garden weed-free. Supply supports to plants that need them.

plant onion sets

Onions are easy to grow from sets (the small, immature bulbs). It is best to buy heat-treated sets because they are less likely to run to flower prematurely than those that are untreated.

1 Onions need an open position in fertile, well-worked soil which has been broken down to a fine tilth (below). Work a little general fertilizer into the soil just before planting.

2 The sets can be planted in drills made deep enough for the tops of the bulbs to be just showing above soil level. Space them 2–4in/5–10cm apart in rows 10in/25cm apart.

3 In fine, very light soil, drills are not necessary—the sets can simply be pushed into the ground at the correct spacing (below). However, on heavier soil, this compresses the soil at the base of the set, making it difficult for the roots to penetrate; the onion sets then push themselves out of the ground.

4 Birds are often a nuisance, tugging the freshly planted sets out of the ground. One way of avoiding this is to trim away the dead, brown leaves at the tip of the set before planting (below) because these dead leaves form a convenient "handle" by which birds can tweak the sets out of the soil.

5 Water the sets shortly after planting if the weather turns dry, and keep them free of competition from weeds. Heat-treated sets are often a little slower than untreated sets to start growing, but they soon catch up.

Onion sets planted in the kitchen garden in mid-spring will provide a good crop later in the same year.

spring
late spring: general tasks

Many soft fruits are now ripening ready for harvesting such as strawberries and currants. To make sure you get the benefits of your hard work, now is the time to protect your crops from birds, which can be a real nuisance at this time of year, as well as the more regular culprits such as slugs and snails.

Protect crops from birds

Much as we like to see wild birds visiting the garden, they become distinctly unpopular when they start wreaking havoc among developing food crops. The soft fruit season will soon be at its peak, and birds are just as fond of the fruits as we are, demolishing them at an amazing speed.

Peas are also at risk from birds: noisy jays are often the main culprits here.

Where possible, protect susceptible crops with netting, ideally in the form of a fruit cage to allow you easy access. Strawberries can be protected with low polytunnels. Or, you can try using bird scarers (see page 85).

strawberry jam
makes 5 x 1-lb/450-g jars

3lb 8oz/1.6kg fresh strawberries, hulled. 3 tbsp lemon juice.
3lb/1.3kg granulated or preserving sugar

Preheat the oven to 350°F/180°C. Sterilize five 1-lb/450-g jam jars with screw-top lids.

Put the fruit in a large saucepan with the lemon juice and heat over low heat until some of the juices begin to run. Continue to simmer gently for 10-15 minutes, until softened. Add the sugar and stir until it has dissolved. Increase the heat and boil rapidly for 2-3 minutes, until setting point is reached. Test the mixture with a sugar thermometer— it should reach 220°F/105°C for a good setting point. Alternatively, drop a teaspoonful of jam onto a cold saucer, place it in the refrigerator to cool it, and then push it with your finger. If it forms a wrinkled skin, it is ready. If not, boil for an additional minute and repeat. Let the jam cool for 15-20 minutes. Skim if necessary. Meanwhile, warm the jars in the preheated oven. Remove and fill carefully with the jam. Top with waxed discs, waxed side down, and screw on the lids tightly. Label and date and store in a cool dry place.

protect fruit from maggots

Most people will have had the experience of biting into an apple only to find maggot damage. The usual culprit is the larva of the codling moth. Chemical control of the moth is difficult, but you can reduce the damage they cause in fruit with pheromone traps. These are hung in the trees and lure male moths to the trap by the use of female pheromones; sticky paper inside the trap ensures that they cannot escape. Such traps were used by commercial growers to indicate the best times to use insecticides, but in the garden they can be used as an effective control.

protect
strawberries

Strawberries are a favorite delicacy for many gardeners but without some timely precautions birds, slugs, or disease are likely to devour them before we get the chance. Now is the time to take action to protect the crop—well before the berries start to ripen.

1 Strawberries are carried close to the ground, making them vulnerable to damp conditions, soil splashes and attack by slugs. This is a good time to surround the plants with clean straw (right) to keep the fruit dry and clear of the soil.

2 Where straw is not easy to obtain, fiber or polyethylene mulching mats or sheets can be used (below, left). They prevent soil splashes and suppress weed growth, but are not so good at keeping slugs and other pests at bay.

3 Many garden birds are extremely partial to strawberries, and the only reliable way to protect the plants is by netting (right). However, because strawberries are so low growing, this is neither difficult nor expensive.

4 There is no point in just throwing netting over the plants because the fruit will still be accessible. Cages are available, or you can make a framework of stakes to support the netting over the plants. Arrange the netting so that it will be easy to remove and replace at picking time.

5 Where birds cause a lot of damage it might be worth investing in a walk-in fruit cage to protect all kinds of soft fruit, such as currants, strawberries, raspberries, and blueberries.

Silver leaf is a common disease of plum trees. Any affected branches should be pruned back until they no longer show a brown stain in the cut wood.

spring
late spring: sowing and planting

Crops in the kitchen garden are growing apace. If the weather is dry, some are likely to need watering to keep them growing strongly, but it's important to know when to water. It should now be safe to sow pole beans in the open without risk of cold snaps.

Flowers on pole bean plants sometimes fall without setting pods. This is generally a sign of dry soil conditions; watering will cure the problem.

Sow pole and dwarf beans outdoors

The soil should now be warm enough for seeds to germinate quickly, and by late spring or early summer, the seedlings should be growing well.

Dwarf beans are sown in single rows, spaced about 3in/7.5cm apart. Pole beans need supports, and they are put in place before sowing; a double row of bamboo stakes, crossing at the top, works well.

There are many varieties of dwarf and pole beans. With dwarf beans, look for varieties that hold their pods well clear of the ground because this avoids beans being eaten by slugs. Purple- or gold-podded varieties are easy to pick because the beans are more visible. Stringless varieties of pole beans are popular because the pods are more tender, and stay in good condition longer.

water vegetables as required

A dry spell can check the growth of young plants, and watering may be necessary. Leafy vegetables respond well, giving an increased yield at harvest time if they have received a steady water supply throughout the growing season. All transplanted vegetables should be watered after planting until they are well established. Other vegetables should not be watered too soon, however, because watering stimulates leafy growth that may be at the expense of flowering and crop production. Beans and peas should be watered once they have started to flower (unless they are wilting) to help the flowers set and promote the formation of tender beans.

top tip

For a fresh and fruity summer salad, mix together 1/6 2oz/500g blanched green beans, with the same quantity of halved strawberries and feta cheese. Add a small bunch of mint leaves and a handful of pistachios and serve with a raspberry vinegar dressing.

plant vegetables in containers

Not everyone has room for a dedicated vegetable plot, but almost every garden has sufficient space for a few vegetables in pots and growing bags on the patio. If the right varieties are chosen, the harvest can be surprisingly good.

When using pots and tubs, ensure they have sufficient drainage holes and place a layer of crocks or other coarse drainage material at the base before filling with compost.

1 Prepare tubs and large pots in the normal way. You can line unglazed terracotta pots with polythene to stop the clay absorbing water from the compost but make slits in the base to prevent waterlogging. The mix can be soil-less or loam-based, as you prefer.

3 Growing bags can also be used for vegetables other than tomatoes (below). A bush-type zucchini plant (one plant per standard bag) will give a good crop, and try pole beans in growing bags placed at the base of fences or walls for the plants to climb up. Both crops need frequent watering.

2 Tomatoes, eggplants (below), cucumbers, and peppers are commonly grown in tubs, and young plants that have been hardened off can be planted out now. Add water-retaining granules to the soil mix to cut down the amount of watering required.

4 Other vegetables that can be tried in tubs or growing bags include potatoes, beet, kohlrabi, carrots, dwarf beans (below), lettuce, and radishes. Choose fast-maturing, compact-growing varieties—there are several that have been bred for growing in pots on patios, courtyards, or balconies.

Zucchini make ideal subjects for a growing bag, but they will need frequent and careful watering.

summer
early summer: general tasks

A range of pests and diseases can ruin the appearance of homegrown vegetables and fruit, but if you act promptly it is possible to protect plants against some of them. If you do not want to use chemical pesticides there are usually more environmentally friendly alternatives available.

Protect fruit against pests and diseases

Codling moth is probably the most troublesome apple pest prevalent at this time of year. The small adult moths fly at night and lay eggs on developing fruit and nearby leaves. When the larvae hatch, they make their way into the fruit and eat their way through it. Pheromone traps (see page 60) give some control, but environmentally friendly insecticides can be used. Look out for gooseberry mildew: it starts as a furry white coating on the shoot tips and young fruits, and soon develops into a dense brown felt on the fruits. A range of fungicides can be used to protect plants.

The dense brown felt that forms on mildewed gooseberry fruits can be rubbed off before cooking, but it is a time-consuming job.

caterpillars and brassica crops

Most gardeners like to see butterflies in the garden but few of them would welcome the cabbage white. It lays eggs on the leaves of any type of brassica, and they hatch out into ravenous caterpillars that can strip a plant bare in a few days. Hand picking and destroying the caterpillars is possible, but not very practical. A better bet is a biological control, which combines spores and toxins from a natural bacteria, and is generally very successful.

earth-up potatoes

When the young shoots of potato plants first appear above ground, drawing soil over them gives protection against late frosts that can occur in areas at risk from frost. As the plants grow, continuing to earth-up prevents toxic green patches forming on the tubers.

1 In cold regions a late frost can still occur in early summer. If potato shoots are just appearing through the soil and frost is forecast, draw up the soil to cover the shoots completely. Alternatively, cover the shoots with sheets of newspaper or row covers held in place with soil or stones, but remove them the following day.

2 As the top-growth develops, continue to draw soil up the sides of the stems at regular intervals to form a ridge (above). This prevents any tubers near the soil surface from being exposed to light that will turn them green; green tubers are inedible as they contain poisonous solanine, which causes severe stomach upsets.

3 As an alternative to the process of earthing-up, potatoes can be grown under black poly mulch. Seed potatoes are planted in cultivated soil and black plastic sheeting is laid over the surface; as the shoots develop, slits are cut in the sheeting in the appropriate positions to allow the top-growth through.

4 The earliest potatoes are usually ready to harvest when the plants begin to flower. Scrape away a little soil to expose the tubers—they are ready to lift when they are the size of an egg (above). Yields are only small at this stage, but these early crops are particularly delicious.

top tip Chilled pea soup is delectable at this time of year. Boil scant 2 cups vegetable stock in a large saucepan then add 1lb/450g fresh peas and scant 3/4 cup chopped scallions. Simmer for 5 minutes, season to taste with salt and pepper, and stir in 1 1/4 cups plain yogurt or light cream.

warm potatoes with pesto

serves 4

1lb/450g small new potatoes. 3 tsp pesto. 1oz/25g Parmesan cheese, grated. salt and pepper

Bring a large saucepan of lightly salted water to a boil. Add the potatoes and cook for about 15 minutes, or until tender. Drain, transfer to a salad bowl, and let cool slightly.

Add the pesto and salt and pepper to taste and toss together. Sprinkle with the Parmesan cheese and serve warm.

harvesting peas

Early sowings of peas should now be ready for picking. They are best harvested as soon as the peas reach a usable size—don't leave them to become too big or they get tough and starchy. Wait until the shapes of the peas are just visible through the pod.

summer
early summer: sowing and planting

The sowing season for vegetables is not yet over. In fact there are several types that can be sown now to extend the season and provide crops in late summer. It's also time to think even further ahead and plant out some of the vegetables that will see you through the winter days.

Sow successional crops

Although the main sowing season is over, there are several vegetables that can be sown successfully over the next few weeks for picking in late summer or early fall. They include radishes, carrots, beet, corn salad, lettuces, kohlrabi, arugula, radicchio, and spinach.

Radishes can be sown at intervals through the summer to provide a succession of roots.

Care should be taken with the choice of varieties as the summer wears on because some are more suitable for late-season sowing than others, being resistant to bolting, or diseases such as mildew. Lettuce often fails to germinate when sown in summer because it is subject to dormancy at high temperatures. This means

lettuce should be sown with extra care in hot spells. Water the drills well immediately before sowing to reduce the soil temperature, and sow in the cool of evening to get the best results.

top tip

You can make a scrumptious salad using mixed salad greens, radishes, tomatoes, cooked beet, red onion, three varieties of canned beans, dried cranberries, roasted cashews, and feta cheese.

plant out winter crops

Winter crops such as Brussels sprouts, cabbages, pumpkins, squashes, and leeks can be planted out now. All brassicas need to be planted very firmly because loose planting leads to loosely formed heads without  a dense heart, and "blown" sprouts. In all but very heavy soils, firm in newly planted brassicas very thoroughly with the sole of your boot; firm again after watering.

plant sweet peppers outdoors

Gardeners in cooler areas can now safely plant tender crops such as sweet peppers, zucchini, cucumbers, and tomatoes outdoors. Make sure the young plants are hardened off before setting them in their final positions.

1 Sturdy young plants that are filling a 3¼in/8cm pot with their roots are the best size for planting out. Select vigorous, healthy plants with deep green leaves; white root tips should be just visible through the drainage holes at the base of the pot.

2 Remove the plant from its pot by placing two fingers either side of the plant's stem, inverting the pot, and gently sliding the plant out of the pot by its stem (left).

3 Dig a hole with a trowel in well-prepared soil in the kitchen garden and set the plant in it (left), covering the top of the rootball with soil and firming in well with your knuckles. Water well after planting.

4 Should the weather turn cool or windy, young plants can be protected by covering them with a cloche (see page 42). As the plants grow, two cloches can be turned on end.

5 Peppers and other tender vegetable crops also grow well when planted in growing bags on a patio (above), often a warmer, more sheltered position. Set two plants per bag for the best results. Cut a cross in the plastic and tuck the flaps under to make the planting hole. Plants in growing bags need regular watering and liquid feeding, particularly in dry or windy weather.

Green peppers are simply fruits picked when immature. If allowed, they will ripen to the other colors.

summer
midsummer: general tasks

There are not too many plant diseases that have a really devastating effect on crops, but potato blight is one of them. Take action as soon as you see the first signs of this disease. Also, tidy up strawberry beds now that the crop is over, and propagate the plants by rooting runners. Check too on outdoor tomatoes.

Potato blight

This disease is common in wet summers, and is remarkable for the speed with which it develops. The first signs are brown blotches on the foliage, sometimes with a white mold on the underside. Symptoms

At the first signs of potato blight on the foliage take immediate action.

spread rapidly, and within a few days the entire top-growth of the potato plants may have yellowed and collapsed.

Blight also affects the tubers, causing a dark brown rot. Spores infect the tubers when rain washes them off the top-growth into the soil. If the tubers are of a usable size,

as soon as blight is identified on the foliage the top-growth should immediately be cut down and burned, removing all trace of it from the soil surface. Tubers may then escape infection.

strawberry beds

When strawberry plants have finished cropping it is time to give the bed some radical treatment. At one time it was common practice to set light to the straw as it lay around the plants; the ensuing blaze burned up the leaves and destroyed any pests and disease spores. Nowadays, the leaves are cut from the plants, using either a pair of shears or a nylon line trimmer: be careful not to damage the new growth in the center of the crowns. Rake up the cut foliage together with the straw, and remove it for burning in a safe place.

root strawberry runners

As long as established strawberry plants are healthy and vigorous, it is easy to produce new plants to extend the bed or to replace old, worn-out plants. Strawberry plants naturally produce a profusion of runners that root quickly and easily.

1 Strawberry runners are freely produced. Long, creeping stolons extend from the plants, bearing two or three plantlets along their length. If not required for propagation, runners are normally removed regularly to prevent a mass of tangled growth (left).

2 Select four or five of the most vigorous runners for propagation and remove the rest. Spread the runners evenly around the plant.

3 The plantlet nearest the parent is always the strongest, and the ones beyond it should be nipped off. Plantlets can be rooted direct into the soil around the plant—simply weight down the runner with a stone or peg into the soil with a loop of wire (left).

4 Alternatively, the plantlets can be rooted into pots filled with either good-quality garden soil or soil mix. Rooting the runners into pots makes the plants quicker to establish on transplanting as there is less root disturbance when the plants are lifted.

train outdoor tomatoes

For a good crop of outdoor tomatoes it is essential to choose varieties specifically recommended for outdoor culture. They may be grown as cordons like greenhouse tomatoes, or as bushes, depending on the variety selected. Cordon varieties need regular side-shooting and tying in to their support, but bush varieties generally do not. Some bush varieties are specially bred for growing in patio pots or even hanging baskets, where the stems cascade over the sides. They need no training, but watering and feeding are necessary.

5 Half-bury the pots in the soil around the parent plant and peg the runners down into the mix (above). When pots are being used, it is important to make sure that the soil mix in them is not allowed to dry out.

Between mid- and late summer, the tops of cordon-grown plants should be pinched out.

Bush varieties form a sprawling mound and do not usually need staking or side-shooting.

summer
midsummer: harvesting and planting

Herbs are valuable in the garden for their appearance and fragrance, and indispensable in the kitchen. While nothing beats the flavor of fresh herbs, there are several easy ways in which they can be preserved. Midsummer, while they are at their peak, is the time to pick them for storing.

Harvesting herbs

The best time to pick herbs is in the morning of a dry day, waiting until the dew has dried off the foliage. Pick young stems, and do not wash them unless it is essential.

The age-old method of preservation is drying; it is simple to do and gives good results. Tie the herbs in small, loose bunches—if they are too large, they will go moldy in the center. Hang them upside down in a warm, dry, airy place. The atmosphere in the kitchen is usually too moist and an airing cupboard (with the door ajar), spare bedroom, or garden shed may be more suitable. Once the stems and foliage are completely dry, the herbs can be crumbled and stored in tightly lidded jars.

For faster results, herbs can be laid on racks in a very cool oven overnight. They can also be dried in batches in a microwave, though it is often difficult to get the timing right with this method.

freezing herbs

Freezing tends to give fresher-tasting results than drying, and is particularly useful for herbs that do not dry well, such as basil.

Pick over the herbs and remove tough stems, then place them (single varieties or a mixture) in an electric blender and almost cover with water. Whiz them in the blender until the herbs are finely chopped, then pour the resulting mixture of herbs and water into ice cube trays and freeze. Add one or two of the ice cubes to soups, sauces, or casseroles.

mint & cucumber refresher

serves 1

few sprigs of mint. 1 tsp superfine sugar. juice of 1 lime. 1-in/2.5-cm piece cucumber, thinly sliced. your favorite sparkling water, chilled

Chop a few mint leaves and mix with sugar.

Rub a little lime juice around the rim of a pretty glass and dip in the minted sugar. Let dry.

Mix the rest of the lime juice, cucumber, and mint—chopped and whole—in a pitcher and chill.

To serve, pour the lime and cucumber into the prepared glass and top off with chilled water to taste.

plant out leeks

Leeks are an invaluable winter vegetable, withstanding almost any amount of cold weather. Seedlings from sowings made in trays or a seedbed in spring will now be ready for transplanting to their final positions.

1 Prepare the ground for leeks thoroughly, because they need to be planted deeply in order to develop the maximum length of tender white stems. The crop will benefit from some well-rotted compost or manure worked into the soil before planting.

2 Loosen the roots, and tease the young plants apart carefully. Gather up a handful of seedlings with the bases of the plants in line, and trim the long, straggly roots and leaf tips with a pair of sharp scissors to make the plants easier to handle (right).

3 Make planting holes some 6in/15cm deep and the same distance apart. Drop a seedling into each hole, leaving the holes open (left). Check the leek drops right to the base: that's why the roots are trimmed back.

4 Once planting is complete, water the plants gently; this washes enough soil over the roots to anchor them in place. Each hole is filled with water and then left to drain (right).

5 If the weather is very dry shortly after planting the seedlings may need to be watered again once or twice, but otherwise they usually need no further attention. They will be ready for harvesting in the fall and winter.

Allow enough space between your rows of vegetables for ease of access when harvesting.

summer
late summer: sowing and planting

The reward for all your work in the kitchen garden becomes apparent as more and more crops are ready to harvest. It's still time to be thinking ahead, however; there are crops to be sown or planted now for next season, and winter crops to look after for the more immediate future.

Spinach for spring

The tender green leaves of spinach make a very welcome vegetable in the spring, and plants sown now are less likely to run to seed than crops sown in the spring for summer use. Traditionally, the prickly seeded varieties of spinach are the ones to sow in late summer and early fall, using round-seeded types in spring. Many modern hybrids are equally good for both seasons, however.

Depending on the weather, there may be leaves to harvest from late fall right through the winter, but the most reliable flush of foliage will be in early spring. Earlier cropping is possible if the seedlings are covered with cloches (see page 42).

(see page 42)

japanese onions

Onion varieties such as 'Express Yellow' and 'Senshyu Semi-globe Yellow' are specially bred for sowing in late summer. They are  winter hardy, and will give the earliest crop next year in early to midsummer. The timing of sowing is fairly critical. Plants that are sown too soon often run to seed prematurely in the spring, whereas those that are sown too late either give a disappointing crop of small bulbs or die out over winter. Gardeners in cold areas need to sow one or two weeks ahead of those in milder areas. Sow in rows that are 9–12in/23–30cm apart, and leave until spring; then thin them to 4in/10cm apart. Water the drills before sowing.

Sow plenty of rows of spinach because the leaves shrink so much when they are cooked.

plant strawberries

The yield and quality of strawberries usually drops off after three years of cropping, and it is advisable to think about replacing one third of the plants in the strawberry bed each year so that you will have strawberries to harvest every year.

1 Strawberry plants are prone to a number of virus diseases that reduce their yields, and it is a good idea to buy certified virus-free stock to give them the best possible start.

3 Well-rooted runners in small pots can be bought from nurseries, or by mail order. They should be planted as soon as possible, spacing them around 12–18in/30–46cm apart in rows 3ft/90cm apart (below).

2 Prepare the soil well before planting, adding well-rotted organic matter and clearing away all traces of weeds, so difficult to control in any well-established strawberry bed.

4 Plant with a trowel (above), firming the plants in thoroughly with your boot. The crown of the plant should be just level with the soil surface. Water after planting, using a medium fine spray on the watering can or hose to avoid disturbing the roots (below).

Crops for harvesting in winter, such as cabbages, should be coming along. Keep them weed free, and water them in dry weather.

summer
late summer: gathering the harvest

In late summer and early fall crops are ripening daily, and much of the produce may go to waste unless it is picked regularly and stored correctly. Some crops need to be consumed as soon as possible after picking, but others will keep for some time provided the right storage method is used.

Harvesting and storing produce

The best time for harvesting is early in the day, before crops lose their moisture in the warm weather. Handle the produce carefully so that it is not bruised; any damaged crops should be kept to one side for immediate use. Once picked, keep the fruit or vegetables for short-term storage in a cool, dark place; the salad box of a refrigerator is usually ideal if there is room.

Root vegetables can be left in the ground over the winter, or stored in boxes of almost-dry mix or in paper sacks. Dense-hearted cabbages, ripe squash, and pumpkins, and many varieties of apples and pears will keep well in a cool, airy shed; onions and shallots can be braided by their tresses into ropes or stored in trays somewhere dry. Don't forget to make jams and pickles, as these are a good way of preserving a wide range of fruit and vegetables.

A good way of storing onions and shallots is to braid the dried leaves together and then hang them up or keep in trays.

freezing

Freezing is probably the most popular method of long-term storage, and is appropriate for soft fruit, or any crop that deteriorates quickly once picked. It preserves the color and flavor of the fruit well, though the texture may suffer in some cases.

Pick over the fruit well; wash it only if essential. It can be open-frozen (ie spread on trays), frozen in containers packed with dry sugar, or frozen in sugar syrup— whichever is most appropriate. Fruit normally cooked (cooking apples and gooseberries, for example) can be cooked before freezing. Remember to label the packs because fruit is difficult to identify once frozen. Most well-prepared fruit will keep in excellent condition for over a year in the freezer.

pruning fruit in summer

Apples and other fruits grown as cordons, fans, or espaliers need to be pruned in the summer to control their growth. Correct pruning is a vital technique for keeping these forms under control so that the plants remain both attractive and fruitful.

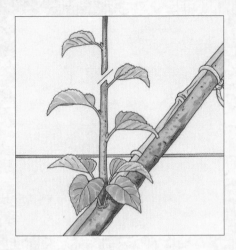

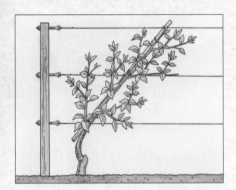

1 Summer pruning should be carried out over a number of weeks as the shoots reach the correct stage. Shoots that are ready for pruning are about pencil thickness, and becoming woody and dark in color at their base (above).

3 The severity of pruning depends on the type of shoot. New lateral shoots that are more than 8in/20cm long and growing from the main stem, should be cut back to three leaves above the basal cluster. Cut just above the bud in the leaf axil, angling the cut so that it slopes away from the bud (above).

4 Side-shoots that are growing from existing laterals or fruit-bearing spurs should be cut back harder, reducing them to just one leaf above the basal cluster. This pruning system improves the cropping potential of the tree by encouraging the development of fruiting spurs, and stopping excessive leafy shoot production (above).

2 The first leaves from the base on each shoot are the basal cluster and usually consist of three leaves. This cluster is ignored when counting the number of leaves on the shoot (above).

apple cobbler
serves 4

½ cup butter or margarine, plus extra for greasing. 3 cups all-purpose flour, plus extra for dusting. 1 cup sugar, divided. 1½ tsp baking powder. ½ tsp salt. 2 eggs. 1 tbsp vanilla extract. 3 tbsp milk. 8 cups thinly sliced peeled baking apples. 2 tbsp quick-cooking tapioca. 1 tsp ground cinnamon

TOPPING

1 tbsp milk. ¾ tsp sugar. ¼ tsp ground cinnamon

Preheat the oven to 350°F/180°C and grease a 13x9-inch/33x23-cm baking pan with butter.

In a bowl, combine the flour, ¼ cup sugar, baking powder, and salt. Cut in the butter until crumbly. In another bowl, lightly beat the eggs and vanilla and add to the crumb mixture. With a fork, gently mix in enough milk to moisten, then stir until the dough forms a ball. Press half of the dough into the bottom of the baking pan. Chill the remaining dough.

Toss the apples with the tapioca, cinnamon, and remaining sugar and place over the dough in the pan. On a lightly floured surface, roll the chilled dough to fit the top of the pan and place over the apples. Brush with milk. Combine the sugar and cinnamon and sprinkle over the top. Bake in the preheated oven for 45-50 minutes, until the apples are tender.

fall
early fall: general tasks

There are sowings and plantings to be made in the kitchen garden, and harvested crops that need to be stored away carefully. Make sure winter vegetables are progressing satisfactorily, and give them the protection they need from the bad weather that may be around the corner.

Harvest pumpkins

In cold regions, pumpkins and winter squash should be cut and brought under cover before the onset of frosts. As long as they are fully ripened, they can be stored for many weeks in a cool but frost-free, dry shed. Check the fruit has no signs of rot or damage, particularly where it has been resting on the soil, before storing.

Maincrop potatoes should also be lifted now. On a dry, sunny day, carefully fork the potatoes out of the soil and leave them on the surface of the ground for several hours to dry. Store them in burlap or heavy-duty paper sacks, or wooden or sturdy cardboard boxes. Do not use plastic sacks; they retain moisture and cause rotting. Store in a cool, dark place and cover the potatoes to exclude all light.

support winter brassicas

Winter brassicas such as broccoli, Brussels sprouts, and various cabbages can make quite tall plants. In exposed gardens they run the risk of being blown over because they have relatively shallow root systems. In windy areas, provide each plant with a sturdy wooden stake.

The earliest varieties of Brussels sprouts will now be ready for picking. Start harvesting from the base of the stem, where the largest buttons are, and gradually work upward.

protect summer-planted potatoes

If you planted a few cold-stored potatoes in summer to give you new potatoes in the fall and winter, you may need to protect the plants from cold weather, depending on the climate in your area. Use a mulch of straw, dry bracken, or similar material along the rows. The first tubers may be ready for harvesting in mid-fall, but in reasonable conditions can be kept in the ground until mid- or late winter.

top tip

Broccoli and blue cheese make a delicious soup. Fry 2 chopped onions in butter, then add a diced potato and a head of broccoli with 4 cups of stock. Cook until soft then blend. Stir in scant 1 cup heavy cream and 7oz/200g blue cheese and warm gently.

lift root vegetables

Some root crops will happily stay in the soil right through winter, but others are best lifted at the end of the growing season and stored above ground, especially in areas where the soil is heavy and inclined to remain wet in winter. Wet conditions are likely to cause the roots to rot.

1 Carrots are at their tastiest pulled young (above) and eaten at once, but maincrop varieties make a useful crop for eating throughout the winter. If left in the soil too long they tend to split, which can make them unusable.

2 Fork up the carrots carefully to avoid spearing them, and shake off loose earth. Cut off the foliage (above), and layer the carrots in boxes of fine, almost dry soil, sand, or peat. Store the boxes in a cool, dark place, eg shed. Use any damaged carrots straightaway.

pumpkin loaf
serves 6

½ cup butter, softened, plus extra for greasing. 1 lb/450g pumpkin flesh. ¾ cup superfine sugar. 2 eggs, lightly beaten. 1½ cups all-purpose flour. 1½ tsp baking powder. ½ tsp salt. 1 tsp ground mixed spice. 2 tbsp pumpkin seeds

Preheat the oven to 400°F/200°C. Grease a 2-lb/900-g loaf pan.

Chop the pumpkin into large pieces and wrap in greased foil. Cook in the preheated oven for 30–40 minutes until tender. Reduce the oven temperature to 325°F/160°C. Let the pumpkin cool completely before mashing well to make a thick paste.

In a bowl, cream the butter and sugar together until light and fluffy. Add the beaten eggs, a little at a time. Stir in the pumpkin paste then sift in the flour, baking powder, salt, and mixed spice.

Fold the pumpkin seeds gently through the mixture and spoon it into the pan. Bake in the preheated oven for about 1¼–1¼ hours, or until a skewer inserted into the center of the loaf comes out clean. Transfer the loaf to a wire rack to cool, then serve, sliced and buttered, if wished.

3 Beet are often pickled in vinegar, but are delicious if cooked like other root vegetables. Unlike the standard red varieties, the golden variety will not stain pink any other food with which it comes into contact.

4 Beet are lifted and stored in the same way as carrots, but the leafy tops should be twisted off, not cut with a knife, to avoid bleeding. Lift the roots before they become too big because they are inclined to go woody (above).

fall
early fall: planting and sowing

As well as harvesting the abundance of crops in the kitchen garden now, keep some continuity of cropping going with further plantings and sowings. A little extra protection from the weather can be gained by sowing under cover. Seedlings from earlier sowings need thinning out or transplanting.

Plant garlic and onions

Garlic can be planted either in mid-fall or in spring but the best bulbs result from a fall sowing. Dig the soil well before planting. Plant each of the cloves in an upright position ¾in/2cm below the soil surface. Space each clove about 4in/10cm apart. If you are planting rows, space each row 18in/46cm apart. Garlic needs good drainage so add plenty of organic matter to the soil and even some sand from a garden center.

Onion sets planted in the fall will give an early crop next year. Varieties for fall planting are chosen for their hardiness and disease resistance, but check that varieties are suitable for your region and climate conditions. See page 59 for details on planting.

thin out seedlings

Seedlings from late sown crops, including lettuce, radishes, and spinach, among others, should be thinned out as soon as they are large enough. This thinning is best carried out in progressive stages to allow for plant losses—thin to half the final recommended spacing first, then remove every other plant later on, as necessary.

Where seedlings are very crowded, great care is necessary to avoid disturbing the roots of those plants that are to remain after thinning.

Fall-planted onion sets and garlic bulbs need free-draining soil so mix in some grit or sand.

lettuce for winter

The pleasure of cutting fresh salads straight from the garden throughout the summer is something that will be sadly missed over the next few months. However, it is possible to have a supply of winter lettuce from the greenhouse; although the plants won't be as succulent and full hearted as summer varieties, they're still worth growing. Sow the seed now; once the seedlings are large enough, they can be transplanted into growing bags, or direct into the greenhouse border.

1 It's important to choose the right variety of lettuce for growing in the greenhouse over winter because not all are suitable. Check with your local garden center to see which ones are the best choices.

2 An unheated greenhouse is quite suitable for growing winter lettuce, although heated greenhouses will give a faster-maturing crop. Cold frames and polytunnels can also be used successfully for growing winter salads.

3 Sow the seed thinly on a prepared flat of moist soil mix (above) and cover lightly. Lettuce seed becomes dormant in very hot conditions, so keep the flat in a well-ventilated and lightly shaded position after sowing.

4 Once the seedlings are showing through, move the flat to full light. Water very carefully to avoid fungus disease. Prick out the seedlings to wider spacings as soon as they are large enough to be handled easily (below).

Transplant cabbages to their final positions. If preferred, space the plants closely to obtain "greens."

fall
mid-fall: general tasks

This is the ideal time to plant new rhubarb crowns. Some soft fruit crops are due for pruning, and hardwood cuttings can be taken to increase or replace stock. Before the foliage of your root vegetables dies back, mark the crop to make harvesting easier.

Plant new rhubarb crowns

Rhubarb is best grown from certified virus-free crowns (also known as sets). They are available from good garden centers or by mail order, and consist of a clump of fleshy roots topped by a knobby crown with one or more large, plump buds.

Dig plenty of well-rotted garden compost or manure into the planting site. Do not add any lime because rhubarb prefers slightly acidic soil conditions. Plant the crowns so that the buds are only just covered with soil; if planting more than one crown, set them 3ft/90cm apart. Do not pull too many stems in the spring following planting. A good and reliable variety of rhubarb is 'Victoria'.

top tip

Plant the herb sweet cicely near your rhubarb, and include a handful of the foliage when cooking the stems. It reduces the acidity, and you won't need to add so much sugar.

If you want to grow rhubarb, make sure that you only buy certified virus-free crowns.

harvesting winter root crops

Root crops such as parsnips can be left in the ground over winter in all but the coldest regions to be pulled as required. However, once the last of the visible foliage has died down there is nothing to show where the roots are. It will save you time and effort if you identify the rows clearly now using a marker. When you start harvesting, begin at one end of the row and move up the marker to indicate where you finished, so that you know where to dig next time.

take hardwood cuttings of soft fruit

Soft fruit, such as raspberries, currants, and gooseberries, are easy to propagate by hardwood cuttings. The cuttings can be left in the open ground all winter, and require very little expertise to root successfully. However, it is most important to remember not to insert the cuttings upside down—it's easier than you might think to make this mistake unless you prepare the cuttings very carefully.

1 Cuttings are taken in the dormant season, using fully ripened wood of the current year's growth. Wait until all the leaves have died before cutting the stems with pruners. Use strong, healthy stems of pencil thickness.

2 Each stem can be cut into lengths to give several cuttings; it may be easy to forget at this stage which end of the cutting is which. Use sharp pruners to cut stems into 6–10in/15–25cm sections, making a straight cut at the base of each length and a sloping cut at the top (above). Treat the bases with rooting hormone.

3 Dig over a suitable piece of moist soil, adding some sharp sand unless it is already free-draining. The cuttings will need to be left in place undisturbed for one year. Make a narrow slit trench with a spade, and insert each cutting so that just the top 2in/5cm is above ground (above).

4 Firm the soil back against the cuttings with the ball of your foot, and label the row (left). Apart from occasional weeding, the cuttings need little further attention. Over winter, corky callus tissue forms over the bases of the cuttings, and new roots should grow from this next spring.

black currants and blackberries

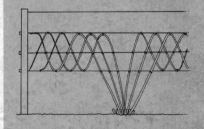

Black currants carry most of next year's crop on the wood that has been produced this season. Cut to the ground all the branches that carried fruit this year, leaving the strong new growths. The older wood can be recognized because it is gray or black whereas new wood is pale brown. If you have trouble differentiating between the old and the new, prune at harvest time next year, cutting out the branches carrying fruit as soon as the currants are ripe.

Blackberries should also be pruned now, again removing the canes that carried fruit but retain the current season's canes. Tie in the canes that are to be retained to their supports. Any damaged, spindly, or weak growths should be removed.

fall
mid-fall: harvesting and digging

Most varieties of apples ripening now are suitable for storing for a few weeks but some will keep until next spring, given the right conditions. In the kitchen garden, digging continues as crops are cleared from the ground. If you do not yet have a vegetable plot, this is a good time to get started.

Harvest apples and pears

A few varieties of apples and pears may need to be left until late fall, but the majority will have been picked by mid-fall. A number of apple varieties store well, in some instances remaining in very good condition until late spring. 'Granny Smith', 'Golden Delicious', and 'McIntosh' are among the good keepers. Choose unblemished specimens, wrap them individually in sheets of waxed paper, and store in a single layer in boxes in a cool garage, cellar, or shed. Or place six apples in a strong plastic bag with a few holes punched in and tie the top loosely, leaving a small gap. Pears do not store well though, and should be eaten within a day or two.

clear vegetable crops

By now, crops such as pole and green beans, summer cabbages, marrows, and so on will be more or less finished, and the plants can be cleared away.

Unless the spent crop plants are badly diseased, add them to the compost heap. Tough, woody stems, like those of some brassicas, are slow to rot so shred them first. As the rows of crop plants are removed, dig the soil over and work in some compost or manure.

Apples are ripe and ready for picking once the stalk separates easily from the spur.

Wrapping apples separately before storing will help to prevent rot spreading if one of them starts to decay. Only unblemished fruits should be stored; damaged apples will not keep.

start a new vegetable plot

Homegrown vegetables are always welcome, and are very rewarding to grow. While a few vegetables can always be grown in containers on the patio or among the flowers, a dedicated vegetable plot will give you a great deal more scope for trying out new, exciting varieties. Make the plot as large as is practical for you to look after.

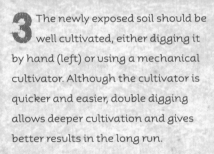

1 If the vegetable plot is to be made in the lawn, it will be necessary to strip off the turf. This can be done by cutting parallel strips in the grass with a half-moon edging iron, and undercutting the turf with a sharp spade (left).

2 If the turf that has been removed is good quality, it can be relaid elsewhere, or perhaps sold. Otherwise, it can be stacked upside down to rot, making an excellent loam for potting or for mixing with growing soil mixes.

3 The newly exposed soil should be well cultivated, either digging it by hand (left) or using a mechanical cultivator. Although the cultivator is quicker and easier, double digging allows deeper cultivation and gives better results in the long run.

4 While digging, incorporate as much compost or manure into the soil as possible; this improves fertility and soil structure, allowing heavy soils to drain more freely and light soils to become more moisture retentive. In cold regions it is enough to leave the plot roughly dug over winter—frost will break down the clods into finer crumbs.

5 A soil testing kit is a worthwhile buy, giving you an idea of the acidity and nutrient levels in the soil (above). Acidity (pH) testing is quite accurate and will indicate whether an application of lime is necessary. Nutrient analysis is less reliable, but will still give a guide to your soil's fertility.

fall
late fall: general tasks

Harvesting the winter vegetable crops usually begins in late fall; protection from hungry wild birds may be necessary. Although many gardeners find the whole subject of fruit pruning mystifying, it can be kept quite simple, and will ensure maximum crops.

brussels sprouts and parsnips

It is said that the flavor of Brussels sprouts and parsnips is improved by a good touch of frost so if your garden is in a cold region it is useful to know that both sprouts and parsnips are hardy enough to withstand even a severe frost without damage, allowing the harvest period to be extended right through winter.

Prune fruit trees

Apple and pear trees that are grown as open-centered bushes or small trees are not difficult to prune. The aim is to maintain a well-shaped tree that carries as much fruiting wood as possible, while also bearing young branches to provide future replacement fruiting wood. First prune out any dead, dying, or diseased branches. Then remove crossing branches, and those growing into the center of the tree. Now cut back strong-growing young laterals (side-shoots) by about half to two thirds of the current season's growth, depending on how vigorous the growth is (the more vigorous the shoot, the more lightly it should be pruned because winter pruning stimulates growth). The tips of the leaders (main branches) should be pruned more lightly, cutting back the current season's growth by about one-quarter. Finally, remove some of the older branches that have borne fruit to encourage the production of new replacement shoots.

lift root crops

Many root crops such as parsnips and maincrop carrots are hardy enough to overwinter in the ground, and will keep in better condition than in store. However, you may need to plan ahead in case conditions turn really cold. Lift a small supply now and store them in boxes of soil placed within easy reach of the house. A few leeks can be stored with them as they too are difficult to harvest in icy weather.

keep birds at bay

A well-planned vegetable plot should contain a variety of vegetables that can be harvested through the winter, but wild creatures will be hungry too, and only too ready to take advantage of a free meal from your garden.

1 Brassicas such as cabbages and Brussels sprouts provide invaluable winter fare, but the plants are prone to damage by pigeons. In a cold spell, a crop can be reduced to a skeleton of veins within hours, so you will need to give it some protection.

carrot soup
serves 8

2 tablespoons butter. 1 onion, chopped. 6 cups chicken broth. 5 carrots, peeled and sliced. 3 small potatoes, peeled and sliced. 1 teaspoon herbes de Provence. 1 pinch dried thyme. 1 bay leaf. Salt and pepper to taste. 8 sprigs parsley

Melt the butter in a large pot over low heat. When the butter begins to foam, add the onion; cook until the onion begins to turn translucent, 3 to 4 minutes. Add the chicken broth, carrots, potatoes, herbes de Provence, thyme, and bay leaf. Season with salt and pepper. Raise heat to medium-high and bring to a boil; reduce heat again to low and simmer until the potatoes are tender, about 30 minutes.

Pour the soup into a blender, filling the pitcher no more than halfway. Securing the lid of the blender with a folded kitchen towel, start to blend using a few quick pulses before allowing to blend continually; puree in batches until smooth. Divide into eight soup bowls; garnish each portion with a sprig of parsley.

top tip

To add some flavor to cabbage, finely shred 1 small white cabbage and cook in 2 tbsp olive oil. Add 2 chopped garlic cloves and continue to cook until the cabbage is just tender. Season well with salt and pepper and add a little chopped preserved ginger before serving.

2 Bird scarers can help to deter pigeons though their effect is often disappointing. Moving, glittery, or noisy objects are best. Strips of foil (above) or unwanted CDs can be hung to shine as they twist in the wind. Tautly stretched tape from old audio or video tapes makes a low hum in the breeze.

3 A physical barrier can be provided by stretching twine between stakes in a crisscross fashion over the top of the crop, or using a horticultural fleece draped over the tops of the plants. The fleece will need to be secured at the edges to prevent it being blown away (above).

4 Growing brassicas in a fruit cage is the most reliable answer where pigeons are a problem. In cold regions, the netting over the top will need to be replaced with large mesh netting to prevent snow from collecting—its weight would tear the net.

fall
late fall: sowing and planting

An out-of-season treat of new potatoes may be available from specially prepared seed potatoes planted in the summer; remember to order potatoes for more conventional planting in spring. It is also time for sowing some vegetables outdoors for next year and planting fruit trees and bushes such as gooseberries.

Sowing beans and peas

Provided you sow the right varieties, both beans and peas will overwinter as seedlings to give crops by late spring. Choose a reasonably sheltered site for sowing, on free-draining soil. On heavy soils there is a risk of the seeds rotting, and in this case it is better to sow them in pots or boxes in an unheated greenhouse for planting out in the spring. The crop will not be so early, but it will be more reliable.

Sow beans 4–6in/10–15cm apart in rows 12in/30cm apart; peas are sown rather more closely in the row, at 2–3in/5–7.5cm apart. Depending on your climate zone and prevailing local conditions, your nursery should be able to advise on the best varieties.

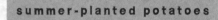

summer-planted potatoes

Specially prepared, cold-stored seed potatoes that were planted in the summer produce a crop some two or three months after planting. Check them now, by scraping away some soil to expose the developing tubers. If the majority are large enough to eat they can be lifted when you want to use them. Do not lift the entire crop as you would for maincrop potatoes; they keep best if left in the soil up to midwinter. A mulch of straw or dry bracken will insulate them from any frost.

Certain varieties of beans can be sown at this time of year to give a crop late the following spring.

plant fruit trees and bushes

With the development of dwarfing rootstocks, it is possible for fruit trees such as apples and pears to be grown even in small gardens. Soft fruit bushes such as currants and gooseberries are similarly easy to grow and provide very welcome crops in the summer.

1 Choose from the wide variety of fruit trees available from specialist nurseries. The plants are often supplied bare root, by mail order, and should be planted as soon as possible after delivery. Most nurseries stock a reduced but reasonable selection.

2 Dig out a planting hole wide enough to take the roots of the tree without cramping, and deep enough for the tree to be planted at the same depth it was in the nursery. Fork over the base of the hole and add well-rotted garden compost or planting mixture.

3 Hammer the stake in position before planting the tree to avoid damaging the tree roots. Check that the size of the hole is correct for the tree, then spread the tree roots out in the base of the planting hole (above).

4 Return the excavated soil to the hole, gently jiggling the tree up and down while you do so to ensure that the soil sifts between the roots. Then you should tread the soil firm with the ball of your foot as you proceed (above).

5 When the hole is refilled, attach the tree to the stake with an adjustable tree tie (left). Soft fruit bushes are planted in the same way. If container-grown, remove the rootball carefully, having watered it well a few hours before, put it in the base of the hole, and firm the soil around it.

potato salad

serves 4

1 lb 9 oz / 700 new potatoes. 8 scallions. 1 cup mayonnaise. 1 tsp paprika. Salt and pepper. 2 tbsp snipped fresh chives. Pinch of paprika, to garnish

Bring a large pan of lightly salted water to a boil. Add the potatoes and cook for 10-15 minutes, or until just tender.

Drain the potatoes and rinse them under cold running water until completely cold. Drain again. Transfer the potatoes to a bowl and reserve until required. Using a sharp knife, slice the scallions thinly on the diagonal.

Mix the mayonnaise, paprika, and salt and pepper to taste together in a bowl. Pour the mixture over the potatoes. Add the scallions to the potatoes and toss together.

Transfer the potato salad to a serving bowl and sprinkle with snipped chives and a pinch of paprika. Cover and let chill in the refrigerator until required.

top tip Gooseberry and elderflower are a great combination for ice cream. Try adding 1 1/2 cups elderflower cordial and 1 tbsp lemon juice to 1 lb 2 oz / 500g pureed gooseberries and mix well. Stir 1/2 cup heavy cream into the mixture and churn in an ice-cream maker.

winter
early winter: general tasks

Continue pruning fruit trees during the dormant season, except when the weather is frosty. Winter digging of the vegetable plot should also be proceeding; it is worth digging the ground as deeply as you can, adding plenty of organic matter to improve the soil.

Protecting beans and peas

Pea and bean seeds sown in the vegetable plot during the fall should have germinated and be showing through the soil by now. Although they are hardy, very cold and windy weather will take its toll of the young plants, so it is worth giving them a little extra protection to see them through the worst spells of winter.

Plants can be protected by glass barn cloches placed over the rows that will keep off the worst of the cold weather and wind, and protect the plants from excess rain. The glass acts as a mini-greenhouse, trapping the warmth of any sun there may be. However, glass cloches are very prone to breakage, and can be dangerous, especially where there are children or pets in the garden. Mini-polytunnels are a safer option, although condensation can be a problem, causing fungal rots to affect the seedlings.

One of the easiest insulating materials to use is lightweight horticultural fleece that is draped loosely over the crop. The edges must be pegged down or secured to prevent the fleece from blowing away in windy weather.

Protect fall-sown beans and pea seedlings from the worst of the weather with mini-polytunnels.

pruning large trees

Most modern fruit trees are grown on dwarfing or semidwarfing rootstocks, but older trees can grow very tall and wide spreading, making pruning difficult. If you use a ladder, have someone at the base to hold it steady. Long-arm pruners make reaching high branches easier; do ensure the blades are sharp and the cutting mechanism works smoothly.

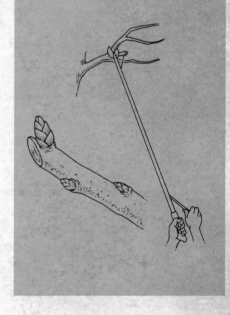

pruning fruit trees

Pruning in the dormant season stimulates strong, vigorous growth the following spring, which is why the major pruning of trees trained as restricted forms takes place in summer. Hard winter pruning of apples and pears grown as cordons or espaliers would only result in uncontrolled growth. Winter pruning on trained trees should mainly be restricted to removing dead, dying, and diseased wood, and thinning out overcrowded spurs.

Plums should not be pruned in the winter because this invites an invasion of silver leaf disease spores. The disease slowly weakens the trees, and forms bracket fungi on affected branches that release spores mainly during the late fall and winter. The spores enter new wood through fresh wounds. Plums should be pruned in the spring and summer when spores are less likely to be around, and in any case the trees more quickly produce natural resins to seal over pruning cuts.

start winter digging

Since digging is satisfying but hard physical work, large plots should be completed in stages to avoid back problems. Digging is best carried out early in the winter, leaving the ground rough for the maximum time to allow frosts to break up the clods of soil.

1 Dig a trench one spit (the depth of the spade's blade) deep across the top of the plot (left). Throw the soil into a wheelbarrow so that it can be moved to the other end of the plot.

2 Chop the soil at the base of the trench with the spade. Move backward and dig a second trench behind the first (below left). Throw the soil from this to fill the trench in front. Try to turn the soil over as you throw it.

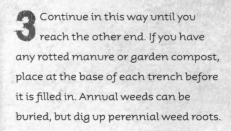

3 Continue in this way until you reach the other end. If you have any rotted manure or garden compost, place at the base of each trench before it is filled in. Annual weeds can be buried, but dig up perennial weed roots.

4 Once the last trench has been dug, fill it in with the soil from the first trench that has been barrowed to the end of the plot. Leave the soil surface rough; repeated freezing and thawing of the moisture in the soil over the winter will improve the soil structure.

winter
midwinter: general tasks

Plant canes and bushes to extend your range of soft fruit, and take action against birds that destroy fruit buds before they even start into growth. Cloches help to prepare the soil for early sowings, but if you can't wait that long, grow your own salad in a preserving jar in a matter of days.

Protecting fruit buds from birds

Various species of small birds can ruin the potential fruit crop of trees and bushes by pecking at the buds on the dormant branches. Every climate zone and local region will have their particular culprits. Apples, gooseberries, plums, pears, and currants can all be affected.

The birds usually eat the tender shoots right in the centers of the buds. Bitter-tasting bird repellents can be sprayed on the trees, while bird scarers also give mixed results (see page 85). The surest way to prevent damage is by using a physical barrier of netting or horticultural fleece.

bushes, canes, and fruit trees

Spells of good weather will allow you to plant fruit trees and soft fruit canes and bushes now.

Extend your range of soft fruits by trying some of the new, improved varieties that find their way into the catalogs every year. Particularly popular are the hybrid berries (which are mainly raspberry/blackberry crosses) such as boysenberry, silvanberry, tayberry, youngberry, sunberry, and veitchberry.

top tip

For a nutritious alternative to mashed potato, cut 1/6/450g peeled parsnips and 1/6/450g peeled carrots into 2-in/5-cm pieces and cook in boiling salted water for 10-15 minutes. Drain well and mash with salt and pepper, butter, and a little grated nutmeg.

Netting prevents birds from destroying a fruit crop or, earlier in the year, the developing buds.

the vegetable plot

In a sheltered place in the kitchen garden, cover an area of ground with cloches to get it ready for seed sowing a little later. Although the cloches might help to trap what heat there is, this is not the sole reason why they are useful at this time of year. Their main purpose is to keep the rain off the soil so that it can dry out, enabling it to be broken down to the fine crumb texture necessary to form a seedbed.

sprouting seeds for winter salads

Winter can be a difficult time to produce fresh salad crops, but sprouting seeds couldn't be simpler to grow. They are ready in a matter of days, and have a pleasant crunchy texture and an interesting range of flavors. Many varieties are also thought to be beneficial to keeping us healthy, with particularly high concentrations of cancer-preventing compounds. A good range of suitable seeds for sprouting is available to order online or from the mail-order catalogs of seed companies.

1 Sprouting seeds can be grown in a wide-necked glass jar topped with a piece of cheesecloth or fine mesh net secured with an elastic band. A square cut from an old pair of tights makes a good cover.

2 Put a couple of spoonfuls of seeds into the jar and cover them with water; allow them to soak for a few hours or overnight. Drain the water off through the mesh on the top of the jar, fill with fresh water, swirl around the jar, and immediately drain the water off again.

3 Place the jar of seeds in a moderately warm position. If they are grown in the dark the sprouts will be white; if they are in the light they will be green and have a slightly different flavor. Every day, fill the jar with fresh water, swirl it around, and immediately drain it away.

4 After a few days the sprouts are ready to eat (right); they will bulk up to almost fill the jar. Among seeds that can be grown are mung beans, alfalfa, and fenugreek; mixtures are also available. Only buy seeds specifically produced for sprouting as many beans are poisonous if eaten raw.

alfalfa & beet salad

serves 4

3½oz/100g baby spinach. 3oz/85g alfalfa sprouts. 2 celery stalks, sliced. 4 cooked beet, cut into 8 wedges
DRESSING
4 tbsp olive oil. 4½ tsp garlic wine vinegar. 1 garlic clove, crushed. 2 tsp honey. 1 tbsp chopped fresh chives

If the spinach leaves are large, tear them into smaller pieces (cutting them would bruise them). Place the spinach and alfalfa sprouts in a large bowl and mix together.

Add the celery and mix well. Toss in the beet and mix everything together.

To make the dressing, mix the oil, vinegar, garlic, honey, and chives in a small bowl.

Pour the dressing over the salad, toss well, and serve immediately.

winter
late winter: general tasks

Dry, breezy days at this time of year can be an advantage: they will dry out the soil and allow you to prepare seedbeds shortly, but if the weather should turn windy and cold, young crops may need some extra protection.

Protecting seedlings

This is still an unpredictable time of year as far as the weather goes—it can produce some of the coldest conditions of the winter, often after a mild spell has already started plants into growth. The young plants of beans and peas that were sown in the fall can be given a severe setback by poor weather now, but they can be protected from the worst of it with cloches or lengths of lightweight horticultural fleece.

Spring cabbage plants not planted out in the fall can now be set out in their cropping positions when the weather is suitable. Like pea and bean seedlings, they can be protected with cloches or fleece should conditions deteriorate after planting.

Thin spinach seedlings to allow plenty of room between each plant as they grow.

Use a fleece (or cloche) to protect pea and bean seedlings against harsh weather.

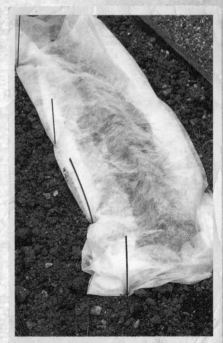

prepare for pole beans

Pole beans are one of the most worthwhile crops for gardeners to grow. They produce a very large crop in relation to the space they occupy, and have an extended season throughout the summer, right up until the first frosts. Although it is a little too early to think about raising the plants yet, it is not too soon to start preparing the soil where they are to grow.

1 Choose a warm, sheltered site for pole beans, preferably moving them to a new position each year to avoid root-rotting fungi building up in the soil. Dig a trench at least one spit deep —or more if you can manage it—and about 2ft/60cm wide. Fork over the soil in the bottom of the trench to break it up (left).

2 Beans need fertile and above all moisture-retentive soil. Adequate levels of soil moisture are necessary to ensure reliable setting of the flowers (the flowers often drop off unfertilized in dry conditions, leading to poor crops), and the rapid development of tender, juicy pods.

3 Add a layer of moisture-retentive material to the base of the trench (above). Ideally this should be well-rotted manure containing plenty of straw but a mix of materials such as grass clippings, fallen leaves, spent mushroom compost, and even old newspapers can be used.

4 Leave the trench open to the rain until it is time for sowing or planting out the beans (after any late frosts in spring if you are in a cold region). Then make sure the base of the trench is thoroughly soaked, by watering if necessary, before returning the topsoil and treading it down thoroughly to firm.

vegetable soup with pesto

serves 6

1 tbsp olive oil. 1 onion, finely chopped. 1 large leek, thinly sliced. 1 celery stalk, thinly sliced. 1 carrot, quartered and thinly sliced. 1 garlic clove, finely chopped. 6⅓ cups water. 1 potato, diced. 1 parsnip, finely diced. 1 small kohlrabi or turnip, diced. 5½oz/150g pole beans, cut in small pieces. 1⅓ cups fresh or frozen peas. 2 small zucchini, quartered lengthwise and sliced. 14oz/400g canned flageolet beans, drained and rinsed. 3½oz/100g spinach leaves, cut into thin ribbons. ready-made jar of basil pesto. salt and pepper.

Heat the oil in a large saucepan over medium-low heat. Add the onion and leek and cook for 5 minutes, stirring occasionally. Add the celery, carrot, and garlic and cook, covered, for an additional 5 minutes, stirring frequently. Add the water, potato, parsnip, kohlrabi, and pole beans. Bring to a boil, reduce the heat to low, and simmer, covered, for 5 minutes. Add the peas, zucchini, and flageolet beans, and season generously with salt and pepper. Cover again and simmer for about 25 minutes until all the vegetables are tender. Add the spinach to the soup and simmer for an additional 5 minutes.

Taste and adjust the seasoning and stir about a tablespoon of the pesto into the soup. Ladle into warmed bowls and serve with any remaining pesto.

seasonal tasks

spring

early spring

Planting/sowing/harvesting tasks

- Harvest rhubarb forced outside or in a greenhouse
- Harvest overwintered crops such as parsnips and leeks
- Sow directly outdoors: carrots, leeks, lettuces, parsnips, summer and fall cabbages, early summer cauliflowers, spinach, and Swiss chard
- Sow into pots in a greenhouse: zucchini, marrows, squashes, dwarf and pole beans
- Chit and plant early potatoes
- Plant container-grown fruit bushes and canes

General tasks

- Finely rake soil in seedbed
- Protect blossom on early-flowering fruit trees
- Support growth of fall-planted peas and beans

mid-spring

Planting/sowing/harvesting tasks

- Sow directly outdoors: beet, Swiss chard, beans, carrots, kohlrabi, lettuces, peas, radishes, scallions, and spinach
- Sow into a seedbed for transplanting later: broccoli, Brussels sprouts, calabrese, cauliflowers, pumpkins, squash, cabbages, and leeks
- Sow melons, cucumbers, tomatoes, peppers, chiles, and eggplants in a greenhouse
- Plant out onion sets

General tasks

- Keep on top of fast-growing weeds
- Support plants at an early stage of their growth

late spring

Planting/sowing/harvesting tasks

- Sow pole and dwarf beans outside
- Plant vegetables such as zucchini into growing bags and other outdoor containers

General tasks

- Keep all plants well watered
- Watch out for signs of pests and diseases on fruit and vegetables and protect crops from birds

summer

early summer

Planting/sowing/harvesting tasks

- Harvest early sowings of peas and beans
- Sow at regular intervals: radishes, carrots, beet, corn salad, lettuces, kohlrabi, arugula, radicchio, and spinach for harvesting in late summer or early fall
- Plant out winter crops such as Brussel sprouts, cabbages, and leeks
- Plant out tender crops such as peppers, zucchini, marrows, pumpkins, squash, cucumbers, and tomatoes

General tasks

- Prune plum and apricot trees
- Watch out for signs of pests and diseases on fruit and vegetables and take action quickly
- Earth-up potatoes
- Prepare beds for new strawberry plants

midsummer

Planting/sowing/harvesting tasks

- Harvest and dry herbs or freeze them
- Transplant tender crops from seedbeds or trays
- Harvest peaches, nectarines, apricots, currants, gooseberries, summer raspberries, and strawberries
- Harvest early potatoes

General tasks

- Watch out for early signs of potato blight
- Tidy up strawberry beds and propagate strawberry plants by rooting runners
- Pinch out the tops of cordon-grown tomatoes to encourage the fruit to ripen
- Keep the kitchen garden as free of weeds as possible

late summer

Planting/sowing/harvesting tasks

- Sow spinach seeds for next spring
- Sow Japanese onions
- Harvest and store summer-maturing fruit and vegetables from kitchen garden and greenhouse
- Harvest plums, fall raspberries, and blackberries

General tasks

- Replace strawberry plants older than three years
- Keep crops for winter harvesting such as cabbages free of weeds and well watered
- Prune fruit trees grown as cordons, fans, or espaliers

fall

early fall

Planting/sowing/harvesting tasks

• Harvest and store pumpkins and winter squashes
• Pick early varieties of Brussels sprouts
• Lift root vegetables such as beet and store
• Plant onion sets and garlic bulbs
• Transplant cabbages to their cropping positions
• Thin out seedlings from late-sown crops such as lettuces, radishes, and spinach
• Sow winter lettuce seed in a greenhouse

General tasks

• Stake tall winter brassicas such as broccoli, Brussels sprouts, and various cabbages
• Protect summer-planted potatoes with a mulch

mid-fall

Planting/sowing/harvesting tasks

• Plant new rhubarb crowns
• Harvest apples and pears

General tasks

• As foliage dies down on root crops, mark the rows clearly
• Take hardwood cuttings of soft fruit such as currants and gooseberries
• Prune out the branches of black currants, summer raspberries, and blackberries that carried fruit this year
• Clear finished pole beans, summer cabbages, and marrows and dig the soil over
• Dig the ground for a new vegetable plot, if desired

late fall

Planting/sowing/harvesting tasks

• Sow peas and beans outside or in a greenhouse
• Plant fruit trees and bushes
• Check summer-planted potatoes and lift any tubers that are big enough
• Lift root crops as needed, especially if icy weather is forecast

General tasks

• Protect overwintering brassicas such as cabbages and Brussels sprouts
• Prune fruit trees

winter

early winter

Planting/sowing/harvesting tasks

• Plant bare-rooted fruit trees

General tasks

• Protect peas and beans sown in the fall with cloches or mini-polytunnels
• Continue to prune large fruit trees and bush fruit
• Dig over the soil in the vegetable beds to allow the frost to break it up

midwinter

Planting/sowing/harvesting tasks

• Cover up rhubarb for early forcing
• Sprout seeds for winter salad
• Harvest winter lettuce from the greenhouse

General tasks

• Cover an area of the kitchen garden with cloches to form a seedbed later
• Protect early fruit buds from birds

late winter

Planting/sowing/harvesting tasks

• Plant spring cabbages in their cropping positions and protect if necessary
• Prune fall raspberries

General tasks

• Prepare the ground for pole beans

Index